KERRY
AND THE
ROYAL MUNSTER
FUSILIERS

KERRY
AND THE
ROYAL MUNSTER
FUSILIERS

A L A N   D R U M M

First published 2010

The History Press Ireland
119 Lower Baggot Street
Dublin 2
Ireland

www.thehistorypress.ie

British Library Cataloguing in Publication Data.
A catalogue record for this book is available from the British Library.

ISBN 978 1 8458 8975 3

Typesetting and origination by The History Press
Printed in Great Britain
Manufacturing managed by Jellyfish Print Solutions Ltd

CONTENTS

ACKNOWLEDGEMENTS

This book, which is based on my MA thesis, is the end result of many months of hard work and could not have been completed without the aid of many people. In particular, I would like to thank my supervisor, Dr Mike Cosgrave, whose patience and ingenuity know no bounds. I would like to thank Gabriel Doherty who, as the course co-ordinator, made himself available and was willing to give a helping hand at every opportunity. I would also like to thank every member of the History Department staff that I have come into contact with over the past twelve months.

My research would have ground to a halt had it not been for the extremely helpful staff of the UCC library, in particular those of the Special Collections Department in Q-1; to them I give a very sincere thanks. To the staff of Kerry County Library in Tralee, Mr Michael Lynch, Mr Tommy O'Connor and Ms Patti-Ann O'Leary, I am hugely indebted. Their expertise and local knowledge is nothing short of phenomenal.

To Noel Grimes and the Killarney War Memorial Committee, I express a deep gratitude. What began as a small local project has grown to such an extent that they have become weighed down by information. My thanks also to my classmates, who welcomed me and aided me with any queries I had.

Most importantly I would like to thank my parents, Breda and Chris Drumm, who have been very supportive and understanding over the past year. I am very grateful to my friends, to whom I promise I will make up for lost time. Finally I would like to thank Miss Sharon Nestor, whose support and encouragement were instrumental and whose patience might be called saintly.

INTRODUCTION

Battles often become the foundation myth for many nations; for Australia it was the needless bloodshed at Gallipoli, for Britain it was Trafalgar and the Battle of Britain, and for Ireland it was the 1916 Rising. Ireland's colonial past is often told in a way that suggests that the sources of British power in Ireland, the RIC and the army, are the instruments of oppression, while the peasant Irish are the oppressed. However, on deeper inspection, many Irishmen enlisted in these security forces and aided in the oppression of other nations and, on occasion, their own people. This makes the 1914-18 period extremely interesting. Ireland had become a willing participant in the Empire, while the Great War was being sold to the Irish people as a war in 'defence of small nations'. To understand this period, we must examine Ireland at a local level, and we must investigate how Gallipoli or the Somme could have been our foundation myth at the expense of the Easter Rising. If we understand this, we will have a far greater grasp of our foundation myth and the events that surrounded the 1916 Rising.

The history of the Royal Munster Fusiliers begins in India with the establishment of a 'guard of honour' by the

East India Company. During the Napoleonic Wars they became known as the Bengal European Battalion, where they fought against native Indians supported by French artillery. After fighting in Afghanistan they became known as the 1st and 2nd European Bengal Fusiliers. In May 1861, after the British Government had taken over the running of India from the East India Company, a Royal warrant was issued upon the Fusiliers. The 1st and 2nd European Bengal Fusiliers now became known as the 101st and 104th Royal Bengal Fusiliers. On 1 July 1881, under the Territorial Scheme, the 101st and 104th Bengal Fusiliers along with the Cork Light Infantry, the Kerry Light Infantry, and the Limerick County Regiments of Militia became known as the Royal Munster Fusiliers. The regimental depot was to be in Tralee, County Kerry.

Prior to the establishment of the Munsters, the Kerry Light Infantry were housed in the ageing Ross Castle in Killarney. In 1810, at the cost of £20,000, a new barracks at Ballymullen was completed. *The Topographical Dictionary of Ireland* describes the barracks, 'about half a mile from the town, and capable of accommodating 17 officers, and 456 non-commissioned officers and privates, and 6 horses, with a hospital for 30 patients, form a substantial building … They stand in an enclosed area about 15½ acres.'[1]

The 1898 Ordnance Survey Map of Ballymullen Barracks shows that a gymnasium and a school had been built within the barracks itself, and to the north-west more houses were built to house soldiers. Located to the south-east is Ballymullen Woollen Mills, and to the south, Castle Desmond Brewery, which no doubt profited from the soldiers in the barracks. The military also located a firing range in the suburb of Ballyard, which is still in use today. It

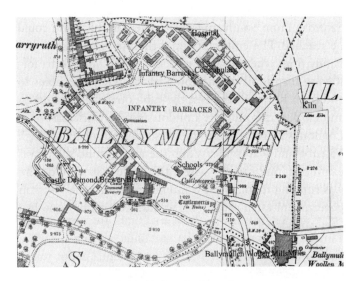

Map of Ballymullen Barracks.[5]

was through Ballymullen Barracks and the firing range in Ballyard that the majority of Royal Munster Fusiliers who served in the First World War passed.

The Kerry of 1914 was often perceived as a backwater of Ireland and the British Empire. John Redmond described Irish farming methods as 'the most simple and barbarous in western Europe'.[2] However 85.6 per cent (or 110,469 people)[3] could read and write, and Kerry had the lowest death rate in the country, at 14.4 per cent per 1,000 of the population.[4] The birth rate was the fifth highest in the country at 23.8 per cent per 1,000. It was also possible to travel from Kerry to any part of the Empire. A would-be emigrant from Tralee could catch the 10.15a.m. train to Cork, arriving at 2.00p.m. From Cork the emigrant could take the 2.30p.m. ferry to Southampton, which left every

Saturday. From Southampton anywhere in the world could be reached. The emigrant could then telegram his or her family from wherever they settled. The red lines in the following map indicate the route of the telegram cables to and from Kerry. To the east the cables travelled to Dublin and Cork and from there London and the world east of it. London was connected to the western hemisphere through Valentia and Waterville. When the area around Valentia is examined, one can see where the cables ran to and who was running them. What is interesting is that the German government ran a cable from Valentia, which by 1906 had been abandoned.

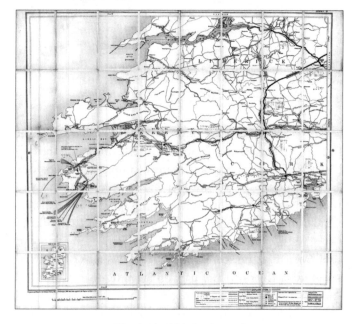

Valentia Island Wireless Station.[6]

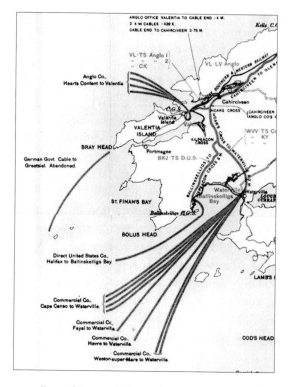

Zoomed-in area of Valentia Island Wireless Station.[7]

Essentially, the area around Valentia in West Kerry was at the centre of a very globalised world. The first map shows that almost every village in West Munster was connected to any location in the world touched by a telegraph cable. Arguably, the Kerry of 1914 was fundamentally as globalised as the world of today. The only real difference is the almost instantaneous speed of email compared to the hours it would take to send a telegram to Sydney, for example.

It is therefore understandable why the German Money Lottery placed advertisements in *The Kerryman*.[8] *The Kerry Sentinel* also placed the results of English race meetings in their paper.[9] It is conceivable that, not only were the people of Kerry able to keep track of racing and lottery results from around the globe using the telegrams, but many other news items. The struggle for Home Rule could be kept track of on a daily basis, as the developments were transmitted to Kerry from London. The death of Sister Theotique Foran from Ballyheigue, who was a missionary in West Africa, was reported in *The Kerry Sentinel* on 24 January 1914. The Reuters Press Agency also had articles on the Mexican War published in *The Kerryman*.[10] Thomas F. Martin notes that ships from Russia, Norway and Sweden docked into Fenit Pier outside Tralee.[11] Martin also examined the manifest books of the Tralee and Fenit Harbour Commissioners from 1928 (all records prior to 1928 were destroyed in a fire) and found that ships docked from ports such as 'Constantinople, Rotterdam and Philadelphia'.[12]

At the outbreak of the war there were fourteen local newspapers in Kerry, plus the two major national daily papers, the *Irish Independent* and *The Irish Times*. Each newspaper had a market and had to be making a profit to remain operating. This paints a picture of a modern Kerry. Adding to the picture is the fact that, in 1915, Tralee and Listowel were connected to the rest of the country by telephone.[13] However, problems remained; the table below shows the number of families living in part of one room, in one room, two rooms, three rooms and four rooms.

District	Part of a room	One room	Two rooms	Three rooms	Four rooms
Killarney Urban	11	83	265	265	168
Listowel Urban	2	111	136	75	86
Tralee Urban	4	266	506	254	300
Cahirciveen	0	346	1,532	1,148	328
Dingle	0	135	943	942	332
Kenmare	0	148	766	617	468
Killarney Rural	2	543	2,097	1,773	627
Listowel Rural	2	375	1,690	1,873	772
Tralee Rural	0	450	1,691	1,761	772

Table 1: Housing statistics in Kerry in 1911.[14]

Indeed a total number of 23,074 people had emigrated from Kerry between 1 April 1901 and 31 March 1911.[15] Thomas F. Martin also writes that 'the majority of farms in Kerry were less than 20 acres'.[16] In spite of these figures, things were improving, but the Great War brought the world to a halt. This book aims to find out how the people of Kerry reacted to the war, and to explain the role they played during the conflict. This book will also explore the role Kerrymen played in the various battles in which they took part, and finally, detail how the ex-servicemen are commemorated both in Kerry and nationally.

I hope that by examining these factors, this book will provide a better understanding of this bloody period in Irish history. I also hope that by writing on this largely neglected period of Kerry's past, I might, in a small way, contribute to the memory of the men who fought and died during the Great War.

The sources I have consulted are local, national and international, with a focus on Kerry-based newspapers from the 1914-1918 period. As there were fourteen newspapers in publication in Kerry in 1914, I examined three to get the best cross-section of the community.

The Kerryman was a weekly paper, which, at the beginning of 1914, was at the extreme end of the nationalist cause. When war was declared *The Kerryman* quickly aligned itself with Eoin MacNeill's Irish Volunteers and after the 1916 Rising shifted its support to Sinn Féin. Maurice Griffen, the editor of *The Kerryman*, was also editor of the twice-weekly newspaper *The Liberator*. *The Kerryman* was closed down by the authorities in August 1916 but continued to print in fits and spurts up to the end of the war.

The Kerry Sentinel was another weekly publication. It represented the middle ground of Kerry society. Although it often leaned in favour of Redmond and the Home Rule cause, *The Kerry Sentinel* also covered the cause of the Gaelic League and many clubs and societies had their notes published in the paper. *The Kerry Sentinel* fell victim to rationing and ceased publishing in 1917 when the owners ran out of paper. Its coverage of the war was unbiased and, in contrast to *The Kerryman*, it published many recruitment posters. Unlike *The Kerryman* it did not continue publishing after the war.

The *Kerry Evening Post* was the paper of the establishment. It was a published twice weekly, on Wednesdays and Saturdays. The *Kerry Evening Post* was openly pro-establishment but it also reported on Home Rule in an unbiased way. By this I mean it reported on the establishment's views on the Home Rule crisis, and often published letters from both supporters and detractors within the establishment.

The *Kerry Evening Post* reported on the various battles in as much detail as it possibly could without fear of censorship. Each publication was accompanied by a number of recruiting advertisements and it became increasingly anti-nationalist as the war continued, in particular after the Easter Rising. It did, however, publish many letters from soldiers at the front and this made it invaluable when I was researching the various battles the Munster Fusiliers fought. Similar to *The Kerry Sentinel*, the *Kerry Evening Post* fell victim to rationing and ceased publishing in September 1917. It did not resume after the war.

In order to extract the best and most relevant information from the various newspapers, I divided each year into various categories. For example I divided 1915 into the categories of economics, war news on an international scale and a local scale, the recruitment campaign, the anti-recruitment campaign and miscellaneous items that caught my eye. This method enabled me to understand the pre-war Kerry of 1914 and to track the changes in the aforementioned categories.

Other sources I gathered to complete this study included *The 2nd Munsters in France* by Lt-Col. Jervis who served in the Munsters as a captain. Originally published in 1922 by Gale and Polden, it was republished by Schull Books in 1998. Jervis compiled accounts from each action the Munsters were involved in on the Western Front. The work of Mrs Victor Rickard, widow of Col. Victor Rickard, who was killed in action at Rue Du Bois, is similar to Jervis's work but only focuses on the Munsters at Etreux, Festubert, Rue Du Bois and Hulloch. General Sir Ian Hamilton's *Gallipoli Diary* is a very insightful source and should be read by anybody wishing to study the Gallipoli campaign. I also examined the surviving service and pension records of the ex-servicemen. These gave me a deep insight into the background of the average recruit and enabled me to increase the number of documented ex-servicemen.

Fortunately, Thomas F. Martin's *The Kingdom in the Empire*, covered much of the ground I intended to study. When I first began researching Kerry's role in the Great War, I read the MA thesis version of Martin's work, *Politics, society, economics & recruitment in Kerry during World War I*. This gave me grounding in the topic and alerted me to the potential ground for original research, specifically the role of soldiers from Kerry during the war. Martin's well-documented work covers everything in relation to the home front in huge detail and so made it easier for me to find the information I needed. The 533 names of dead servicemen he collected I found particularly helpful in building up statistics.

The past eighty to ninety years have created many myths in relation to Irish involvement in the First World War. At first, many regarded the ex-soldiers as traitors to the state, and in the early years of Irish revisionism they were regarded as the real heroes of the revolutionary period. Because of this, there are many contradictions in the modern perception of Ireland's involvement in the conflict. It is therefore up to the modern historian to scrutinise all previous works and come up with an impartial view that does not follow an agenda on such a divisive topic as Irish involvement in the First World War.

WHY ENLIST?

At the turn of the twentieth century Ireland was a largely pacified country. The failure of the 1798 Rebellion and the trauma of the Great Famine brought a shift in attitudes. Irish people both supported and held a firm belief in Home Rule and the Irish Party under John Redmond. Although there was still a physical force element in Irish society, it remained diminutive and consisted of small secret societies. One of these was the IRB, whose membership numbers in Ireland and Britain was 'down to between 1,500 and 2,000'[17] by 1910. By the outbreak of the Great War Redmond was at his peak. Home Rule was on the verge of implementation and the majority of Irish farmers owned their lands after the passing of the various Land Acts. Only a catastrophe could stop Home Rule becoming a reality before 1915.

That catastrophic event occurred when war was declared on 4 August 1914. It was clear from the outset that the standing British Army was too small to fight a war on the continent and protect her immense empire. Lord Kitchener planned to raise three new Irish Divisions: the 10th and 16th (Irish Divisions) and the 36th (Ulster Division). The 10th Division was made up of both nationalists and unionists, as

Major Bryan Cooper, a unionist from Dublin, wrote in his book *The Tenth (Irish) Division in Gallipoli*:

> Many of the officers and men had played, or, at least, had relatives who had played, an active part in the agrarian and political struggles that have raged in Ireland for the last forty years. Yet all this went for nothing, the bond of common service and common sacrifice proved so strong and enduring that Catholic and Protestant, unionist and nationalist, lived and fought and died side by side like brothers. Little was spoken concerning the points on which we differed, and once we had tacitly agreed to let the past be buried we found thousands of points on which we agreed … It is only to be hoped that the willingness to forget old wrongs and injustices, and to combine for a common purpose, that existed in the 10th Division, may be a good augury for the future.[18]

The 16th Division was predominately nationalist and Catholic, while the 36th Division was largely made up of unionists and Protestants. These Irish Divisions were to be filled by men of both the UVF and IVF. Kitchener and the War Office decided against having distinct Irish divisions, instead opting for the numerical system used by the army.

Redmond and the majority of Irish people supported the war effort, and Redmond even proclaimed to Parliament that Britain, 'may take their troops away, and if it is allowed to us in comradeship with our brothers in the North we ourselves defend the coasts of Ireland'.[19] Redmond was supported in his plea that Ireland be defended by the Volunteers by Bryan Cooper. He telegraphed Redmond to say, 'Your speech has united Ireland. I join the National Volunteers today, and will urge every unionist to do the same.'[20] However the appeals of Cooper and Redmond were turned down and Ireland was to be defended by the army.

In County Kerry the home regiment were the Royal Munster Fusiliers and it was to this regiment the majority of Kerrymen would enlist. At the outbreak of the war the Munsters were four battalions strong – two regular and two reserve. These four battalions were joined by a further seven during the course of the war. The exact number of Kerrymen who enlisted in the army is unknown, as the documents that contained this information were destroyed during the London Blitz. Thomas F. Martin put together a list of 390 officially recorded Kerrymen who died during the war, and a further 143 who were not officially recorded or died in the service of other Allied Armies. I assembled a list of 264 who fought and survived the war, and so together we have assembled a list of 797 names. Martin suspects that the list of casualties may be closer to 600[21] and taking all these figures into consideration, I suspect that as many as 2,000 Kerrymen participated in the conflict.

ECONOMICS

The most common and most discussed reason for enlistment on a national level as well as on a local level is economics. The Kerry of 1914 was not the most prosperous part of the United Kingdom. Housing conditions were appalling as Murray Fraser points out. 'In south-west Munster, hearths were central, and in most cases a dairy was attached. Elevations were of plain, rendered masonry walls and of simple slate roofs to ward off the harsh western climate.'[22] The Kerry County Committee of Agriculture scheme of prizes for cottages and small farms in 1914 reported that 'in some of the older cottages earthen floors still exist in kitchen and bedrooms, rendering the house damp and unhealthy'.[23] However, those who lived in local-authority housing lived in much better conditions, as the article continued, 'the District Council cottages were on a whole, very comfortable and fairly well kept'.[24] In Tralee the building of local authority housing was in such high demand that thirty-eight were built in 1913 and a further thirty-nine were due to be built in 1914.[25] For the poor of Tralee, seventy-seven new affordable houses in two years was not enough. These housed some of the 159,961 people recorded in the 1911 census.[26] Most of these people lived off the land, but in 1914 Kerry and the Munster region in general suffered from a foot and mouth outbreak. Therefore an embargo was placed upon the province which severely restricted the movement of cattle out of Kerry. In 1914 the Puck Fair, the largest fair in the county, reported 'very little sale of cattle in any section and these, generally, went home without changing owner'.[27] The lack of the livestock trade in Kerry occurred when prices for cattle in England were up from $7.5d$ per lb to $8d$ per lb.[28] This meant that the 288,998 cattle[29] in the county were grazing when there were high prices and high demand in England. As there was no money to be made at market, farming throughout the summer of 1914 became a struggle. This may have forced many young farm hands and labourers into the army.

As the foot and mouth crisis was coming to an end and as restrictions were finally lifted on 4 July 1914, the Tralee and Fenit Harbour Commissioners began to debate the pros and cons of exporting cattle. The Harbour Master had applied for a grant of £5,000 to build a jetty, via local MP Thomas O' Donnell. However, as the Limerick Steamship Company pointed out, 'Fenit is 186 miles farther from Liverpool than

Waterford, and 180 miles farther from Bristol than Waterford. That again, Fenit is farther from Liverpool by 130 miles than Cork, or 139 miles than Bristol.'[30] During this same period the Western Railway Company was complaining that 'the facilities for loading the ships were far greater than the facilities for discharging the wagons at Tralee'.[31] This should have put an end to the plan, as there was not enough space in Tralee to load and unload the cattle. The authorities of the time would have been better off developing rail heads in Tralee, Listowel and Killarney, so as to make it easier to send cattle to the main exporting ports in Limerick and Cork.

When Britain declared war, her department of agriculture placed advertisements in *The Kerryman*. The department asked farmers to grow 'catch crops' such as wheat, oats and even cabbage. This came at a time when only 597 acres of Kerry was under wheat, 22,875 acres under oats, 1,952 under barley and 352 acres under rye. When other crops such as potato and cabbage are included, the total amount of land in Kerry under crops was 180,595 acres from a total of 1,161,752.[32] This was, in essence, a transition to a labour-intensive method of farming. The men the army could have recruited in Kerry due to the foot and mouth crisis might now be involved in this new transition. This may have been one reason why young Irish farmers were so reluctant to enlist. It must also be noted that it was possible for young farmers to emigrate to America, Australia and Canada. Advertisements were placed in all the local newspapers offering 160 acres to possible *émigrés* if they left for Australia.[33] They also offered reduced passages of £6 for farmers and farm workers.[34] Women were also needed in Australia, and were offered positions as domestic servants and a reduced passage of £3.[35] Canada offered 160 acres[36] to potential *émi-*

grés, while the province of Winnipeg was looking for anyone from railway workers to farm hands. The state of Idaho in the USA offered young Irish people 40 to 160 acres, provided the *émigré* had £250. They also promised that 'wages in Idaho, Wyoming, Nevada, Utah and adjoining states are seven times higher than in Ireland'.[37] Tom Johnstone states in *Orange, Green and Khaki* that, 'rural England found it as difficult to raise its quota as rural Ireland'.[38] With what was on offer at the time, it is no wonder rural men did not enlist in the numbers that their urban counterparts did.

Although it may have been seen as a gamble, most of the recorded relocation advertisements were placed in the press during wartime, thus giving another option other than joining the army. These advertisements were aimed at farmers' second sons of Kerry; they would have read and witnessed how the various Battalions of the Royal Munster Fusiliers were wiped out in France and Gallipoli. The choice for these young men was stark – fight in the mud of France, toil on the family farm with no opportunity to own it, work in the munitions factories of England, or emigrate and take a chance in the 'new world'.

In urban areas such as Killarney, Listowel and Tralee, the situation was somewhat different. Killarney relied on the tourist industry as much then as it does now. *The Kerry Sentinel* noted that:

> …certain classes of workmen in Killarney, such as boatmen, jarveys, etc, are suffering in consequence of a very bad tourist season, and they stated that the present war was primarily the cause … There can't be any question about it at all, we have had no tourist season in Killarney this year; the waiters have been dismissed, jarveys have had to sell their horses and the families of the poor are weak with hunger.[39]

The drop in tourist numbers came following a period of high investment in the tourist industry; £21,450 had been invested in the roads of the county during 1913/1914[40] and one private individual had invested in an expensive large vehicle, named the 'The Killarney Express'.[41] More investment had been made, as the *Kerry Evening Post* reported that some:

> ...have complained of the poor hotel accommodations and railroad facilities that existed some years ago. During a recent visit there I found that all this had changed. Not only in Killarney, my native town, but throughout Ireland ... I found the same improvements had been made everywhere ... Killarney is one of the prettiest spots a tourist could choose to visit ... and that Glengariff is another of the best known health resorts.[42]

The *Kerryman* also reported a tourist industry in Waterville which revolved around the fishing season and the 'Grand Atlantic Route', which brought tourists to the town.[43]

However, more investment was needed. The Dingle Peninsula was in special need of attention as 'the absence of an efficient water supply and sewerage arrangements is a great drawback and will militate against the natural development of Dingle town and district as a tourist resort'.[44] Dingle was not the only urban area suffering from a poor water supply. Listowel, which in 1914 was viewed as 'the capital of North Kerry'[45] was negotiating with the Electrical Lighting Company for a new waterworks facility. The new facility would allow Listowel 100,000 gallons of water per day or 30 gallons per head, which, according to the article, was the number allowed in Liverpool and Manchester.[46]

The urban–rural divide was summed up by *The Kerryman*:

...if the war did a kind turn for the cattle trade, it has had a disastrous effect on Irish tourist traffic. Things are as bad as bad could be, in our principal tourist resort, Killarney, where some families who were mainly dependent on the tourist traffic are almost on the starvation line, and with prices on the increase, the outlook for those poor people is untruly disheartening ... Reports have come to hand that in Waterville, Kenmare, Ballybunion, Dingle and other beauty spots, the tourist traffic is as dead as it is in winter.[47]

The removal of the foot and mouth restrictions, the natural increase in prices of agricultural goods, the move to labour-intensive forms of farming, and better opportunities abroad are the reasons why the rural men of Kerry did not flock to the recruiting offices. For the men of urban Kerry, whose opportunities were already limited prior to the war and were now almost non-existent, the war offered economic opportunities not only for the prospective soldiers, but also for their families, in the form of a separation allowance. These facts not only show why urban-based men enlisted in far greater numbers than their rural peers, but also show why recruitment began to tail off in 1915. After the initial surge in recruitment there were simply not enough willing recruits to replace those who were lost at the front, because they simply did not have to.

HOME RULE

Another popularly mooted reason for enlistment is the belief in and support for the Home Rule cause. The House of Lords stood in the way of the 1883 and 1886 Government of Ireland Bills, and until the 1909 Parliament

Act it seemed they would forever stand in the way. The Parliament Act curtailed the power of the Lords. Their unlimited power to veto was reduced to a veto of two years on Bills which had been rejected twice by the Lords. The door was now opened to Home Rule, provided that Redmond held the balance of power. The opportunity arose when the Irish Party held the balance of power after the 1910 General Election. The Home Rule Party won all four seats in the four constituencies of Kerry. In Kerry North, Michael Joseph Flavin was elected, in Kerry West, Thomas O'Donnell, in Kerry South, John Pius Boland, and in Kerry East, Timothy O'Sullivan. The 1912 Government of Ireland Bill was passed by the Commons but rejected by the Lords. However, due to the Parliament Act, Home Rule was due to become law in 1914.

The reaction in nationalist Ireland was one of jubilation, while unionist Ireland reacted by signing the Ulster Solemn League and Covenant in September 1912. In January of 1913 the Ulster Volunteer Force (UVF) was established. The UVF then armed themselves, in clear defiance of the British authorities, after landing arms at Larne in April 1914. Nationalists in return established the Irish Volunteers on 1 November 1913, and they landed arms in Howth.

The pace of events that preceded Britain's declaration of war on 4 August 1914 took many people by surprise. The Archduke Franz Ferdinand had been assassinated over a month earlier on 28 June. For the general public of the British Isles the crisis was 'over there'. But as Europe began arming itself for a conflict involving all the major nations, Ireland was already armed and in danger of becoming embroiled in a civil war. The two private armies eyed each other up, and in Kerry, Thomas O'Donnell, on 6 June 1914, called on the men of Kerry to show 'their spirit of patriotism which ought to make everyman, from sixteen to sixty a soldier in the ranks of an Irish Army'.[48]

Redmond and the Home Rule leadership had no doubts about how Ireland should react to the European war. Ireland was to support Britain by encouraging its young Irishmen to fight for Britain, but they would ultimately be fighting for Ireland and Home Rule. Some did not support Redmond's stance on the war. This led to a split in the Irish Volunteers; Redmond and his supporters formed the new Irish National Volunteers, while Eoin MacNeill's anti-war group continued using the title of Irish Volunteers.

When war was declared the Irish leadership changed tact; they would support the war effort and get the best possible deal for Home Rule. In a speech to Parliament Redmond declared:

> For the first time in the history of the connection between England and Ireland, it was safe today for England to withdraw her armed troops from our country, and that the sons of Ireland themselves, North and South, Catholic and Protestant, and whatever the origin of their races may have been.[49]

The *Kerry Sentinel* reported that Volunteers would be armed and organised as part of the new army.[50] The report was given more weight when General Sir Bryan Mahon visited Tralee to 'ascertain the strength and general status of National Volunteers'.[51] Reports such as these would have undoubtedly helped recruitment, as Kerrymen would be fighting for an Irish Army. This plan was rejected by Kitchener and later criticised by John Robert Godley, the Under Secretary of State for War:

I have always thought that if those in authority had the vision and the foresight in the early stages of the war, to raise three divisions in Ireland – one in Belfast, one in Dublin and one in Cork – and to turn them into an Irish Army Corps under the command of John Redmond, the history of my distressful country might have been very different ... And what a nucleus for that corps would have been, all the splendid Irish regular regiments with their glorious records and traditions. But the English politicians, and I am afraid, many English soldiers, were totally unable to understand Irishmen. They would not trust them.[52]

Many people in Ireland, like the peoples of Europe, were caught up in war fever. An Irish Army Corps led by an Irish general such as Galway's General Mahon would have been a recruiting coup. The Volunteers may have split but it would have been very difficult for nationalist Ireland to turn down an Irish Army, whose leaders had just won Home Rule. *The Kerry Sentinel* picked up on this, 'it would be an irreparable blunder if British statesmanship failed to seize this great opportunity for a genuine peace and reconciliation between Ireland and the Empire'.[53]

The Kerryman led the anti-enlistment campaign in the county. They informed their readers that:

...instead of getting Home Rule, we are treated by the cabinet to the masterly expositions of equivocation and delay. In the meantime, we are frantically urged to fight for the Empire ... When we get Home Rule, it will be full time enough to ask Irishmen to do their part of the fighting ... During the progress of England's wars with Napoleon, Irish Catholic soldiers laid down their lives for the Empire by thousands while their co-patriots were refused the ordinary rights of citizenship.[54]

It is easy to see why some people did not trust the British authorities. Apart from the historical differences, MacNeill and his followers in the Irish Volunteers may have foreseen that a drawn-out war could bring a change of leadership and change in attitudes towards Home Rule. Remaining in Ireland to protect the implementation of Home Rule was not such a ridiculous concept. Their support, small at first, grew as the war continued. This swell of support may have more to do with disillusionment with the war and a way of expressing concern over conscription.

It is easy to understand why young men would join the British Army because of their support for Home Rule; nevertheless it is also easy to understand why people would distrust the British Government, given their past injustices. In 1914, neither Redmond and MacNeill could possibly have known what was going to happen. Redmond was at the peak of his powers; in achieving Home Rule he had taken over the mantle of 'King of Ireland' from Parnell. Redmond could not but support Asquith and the war effort. Others such as MacNeill could afford to theorise about supporting the war effort. However MacNeill certainly did not know in 1914 that he would be involved in the Easter Rising. MacNeill's choice was a political decision based on nationalism rather than republicanism.

MILITARY TRADITION

There was a strong military tradition in Kerry, after the establishment of the Royal Munster Fusiliers and their regimental depot in Tralee. Services associated with the military barracks sprung up around the town. Houses were built in

Ballymullen and Moyderwell for the soldiers. The Munster Bar (so named because the Munster Fusiliers drank there) and a creamery were built in Ballymullen. There is no doubt that Tralee benefited from having a regimental depot in the town. There is also no doubt that the people of Tralee and Kerry fought in large numbers in every British military campaign from 1881 until 1922. Kerrymen took part in the Crimean War (1853-56) and are commemorated on two cannons outside the Tralee District Courthouse. The 1st, 2nd and 5th Battalions of the Munsters served throughout the Boer War and are commemorated on the Royal Munster Fusiliers memorial in Killarney.

Military tradition is something associated with the Protestant landed gentry in Ireland. Nevertheless three battalions of the Royal Munster Fusiliers served in South Africa twelve years before the First World War. Pressure from older brothers, fathers and uncles may have forced many young men into the army. Tom Barry alluded to this rite of passage in *Guerrilla Days in Ireland*, 'I knew nothing about nations large or small. I went to the war for no other reason than that I wanted to see what war was like, to get a gun, to see new countries and to feel like a grown man.'[55]

There is a strong military link between Britain and Ireland. According to David Murphy in *The Irish Brigades 1685-2006*, Irishmen have joined British regiments since 1685 and the tradition continues to this day in the form of the Royal Irish Regiment. *The Kerryman* newspaper, although representing republican opinion until 1916 when the authorities closed it down, reported in detail on the Royal Munster Fusiliers' exploits. One gets the feeling that despite the fact Kerrymen were in the service of the Crown, they were still our regiment and something to take pride in.

The armed forces also offered many young men the opportunity to travel. 'Join the navy and see the world' could not be a truer statement. The Royal Navy's Mediterranean fleet had bases in Alexandria, Malta, and Gibraltar amongst others. The Home fleet was stationed in Dover and Scapa Flow and the main base for the fleet in the Far East was in Singapore, with others in Australia and India. The navy was not the only division of the armed forces that allowed young men to travel. The 1st Battalion of the Royal Munster Fusiliers were stationed in India prior to the outbreak of the First World War and the regiment has Battle Honours from Afghanistan, India and South Africa.

The Armed Forces of the United Kingdom have always offered young Irish men the opportunity to search for adventure. David Murphy claims that in 'the mid-nineteenth century, somewhere between 35 and 40 per cent of the British Army was composed of Irishmen'.[56] Adventure of course was not the only reason why Irish people were in the service of the Crown. Economic conditions forced young men into the army, others willingly joined because it was a family tradition. *The Old Kerry Journal* claims that Tom Crean may have been influenced by 'the large-scale naval manoeuvres, which were held off the west coast of Ireland, including Dingle Bay, in the Summer of 1892'.[57] Crean enlisted in 1893 and went on to become a famous name in Antarctic exploration. Who is to say that others were not influenced by those naval manoeuvres and others involving the army?

These are some of the over-arching reasons why men enlisted in the army. Because conscription was never introduced in Ireland the authorities had to persuade people to enlist. Therefore we must examine the recruitment campaign, the tools and propaganda, and the role played by the local recruiting agents. We must also examine the anti-recruitment campaign and the role played by Sinn Féin and MacNeill's volunteers in order to observe how the authorities reacted to the developments in Irish opinion towards the war.

RECRUITMENT

When war was declared on 4 August 1914, it caught many people by surprise, including the British Government. Publicly they spoke of a short war but privately they prepared for a long one. Lord Kitchener of Listowel was charged with recruiting the new citizen armies that would fight what would become a World War. The task facing Kitchener was nothing short of colossal. After the reversals during the Boer War, the British Army underwent a radical overhaul. Despite this, the British Army remained a small force in comparison with those of the other major powers. Kitchener not only had to attract young men into the colours but also train them into an effective fighting force. Attracting the young men of Kerry was going to be a completely different proposition to recruiting the young men of England. A different strategy would be needed to tackle the political and economic situation in Ireland.

Tralee, unlike the other large towns in Kerry, had a long-established link with the British Army. Ballymullen Barracks was the depot of the Royal Munster Fusiliers. The 1911 census recorded 9 officers and 149 NCOs and other ranks living in the town. This compared to one NCO or soldier living in Listowel and one officer living in Killarney.

Their economic and social contribution would have raised the profile of the army in Tralee, making recruitment easier. This evidence is borne out in Table 2, which shows where the men who were killed in the conflict were from.[58]

Table 3, compiled from the available service records, also bares the fact that most of the would-be recruits were from urban Kerry and in particular Tralee.

It was clear from the outset of the war that the economically disadvantaged would be among the first to enlist, and would provide a steady stream of recruits as rising poverty caught up with others. In September 1916 the *Kerry Evening Post* reported that food prices had increased by 60 per cent and 'that the purchasing power of the sovereign has been reduced to 12s 6d'.[59] Adding to the problems of the ordinary people of Kerry, there was a massive decrease in potato production, 'The total production in 1916 was 85,871 tons against 119, 405 last year … The decrease in the total production in Kerry was no less than 34,034 tons or 28.5 per cent.'[60] Further adding to the people's difficulties were the record prices that were being recorded at fairs throughout the county – at the Tralee Pig Fair prices were said to have 'gone mad'.[61] Things were to get worse for the people on the Dingle Peninsula. The County Council could no longer run the train service on the peninsula or continue to relay railway sleepers due to the 'increased price of coal, and the absolute impossibility of getting sleepers'.[62] This in turn led to 'twenty to thirty men thrown out of work, and they had families which altogether, might mean forty or fifty people'.[64]

For the farmers, inflation meant increased prices for their produce. Kerry Co-op released the figures in the press detailing their profits from 1908 to 1915 (Table 4).

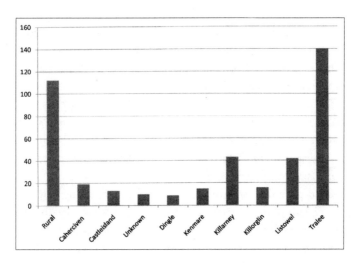

Table 2. Hometowns of those who died in the conflict.[58]

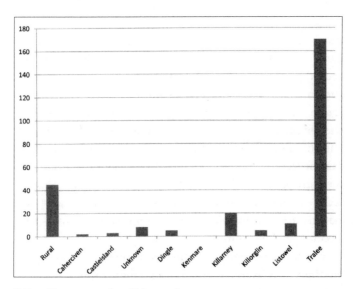

Table 3. Hometowns of would-be recruits.

Year	Sales	Net Profit
1908	£4,401 8s 11d	£134 15s 5d
1909	£11,572 14s 4d	£203 4s 3d
1910	£12,914 9s 8d	£231 2s 8d
1911	£14,672 18s 2d	£259 5s 1d
1912	£16,205 12s 2d	£260 19s 9d
1913	£17,112 1s 6d	£255 4s 10d
1914	£19,836 15s 1d	£344 18s 2d
1915	£19,000	£343

Table 4: Profits for Kerry Co-op, 1908-1915.[64]

The high prices and profits meant that many farmers could begin investing in their farms following the foot and mouth crisis of 1913/14. The Kerry County Committee of Agriculture in 1916 reported that 'commendable mention must be made as to the efforts taken to conserve the liquid manure of the farm. Many new cement receptacles were seen for the purpose of collecting this liquid.'[65] In the farm section of the report the committee stated that, 'in many cases the dwellings seemed to be recently improved by the addition of good cement floors, rooms and kitchens neatly ceiled and the addition of larger extra windows improved the comfort and healthiness of the houses'.[66]

Farmers were not only investing in their homes. Table 5 below shows the increase in livestock kept in Kerry from 1914-16.

Year	Cattle	Horses	Sheep	Pigs	Goats
1914	288,988	18,948	120,791	79,927	15,061
1915	274,360	16,781	122,459	66,632	13,690
1916	283,569	19,079	113,710	75,284	17,929

Table 5: Livestock Statistics 1914–1916.[67]

Year	Acres
1914	180,595
1915	181,525
1916	184,438

Table 6: Land under crops 1914-1916.[68]

In 1915, livestock numbers decreased. There were two main causes for this; high cattle sales at the onset of war, and the foot and mouth crisis of 1914, when there would have been cattle grazing but not for sale until 1915. Farmers did not increase crop production dramatically, contrary to Government requests for the duration of the war. Table 6 shows the acreage of land under crops in Kerry.

The high price of livestock was a disincentive to grow crops, which in turn reduced the labour requirement. Army recruitment was aided considerably as urban men had no employment opportunities as farm labourers. This economic situation created a divide in Kerry. Rising inflation was squeezing the urban working class, whose opportunities now lay with the army, and farmers were becoming increasingly wealthy. This divide is shown in the tables describing where the recruits were from and their occupations. The table shows that 123 men out of the available 264 available in service records were labourers. It was these men that would have been hardest hit by the rising prices. Forty-two are tradesmen, who probably enlisted because there was not enough money available to complete the various work schemes around the county. This fact is backed up by figures published in *The Kerryman* regarding unemployment amongst tradesmen in Tralee, as shown in Table 8.

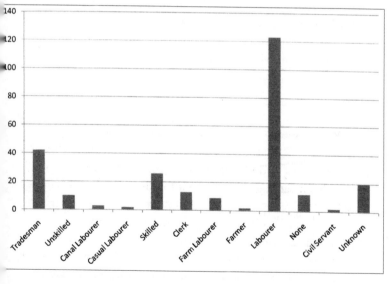

Table 7: Occupation of recruits.[69]

Trade	Number of Unemployed in 1915	Average number of Unemployed the previous winter of 1914
Painters	30	12
Masons	35	6
Stonecutters	6	2
Plasterers	10	0
Builders/Labourers	20	0
Carpenters	10	0

Table 8: Number of unemployed tradesmen in 1915.[70]

What was happening to the people of Kerry was a form of economic conscription. Men who did enlist could take solace from the fact that their families would receive a separation allowance from the government. The amounts of money are shown on Table 9.

Dependents	Corporal or Private family, allowance per week	Sergeant family, allowance per week
Wife	12s 6d	15s
Wife and one child	17s 6d	20s
Wife and two children	21s	23s 6d
Wife and three children	23s	25s 6d

Table 9: Separation Allowance. Two shillings more was received for every additional child.[71]

Attempts were made to create employment. Thomas O'
Donnell MP attempted to obtain government funding for
a glass-manufacturing plant in Tralee. The County Council
also applied to have an arms factory established, but both
these attempts failed to get off the ground. This was the
backdrop to which recruiting sergeants tempted young men
into the army. Politics, however, was to influence Kerrymen
as much as economics.

When war broke out, Kerry's support for John
Redmond was unwavering. He had all but achieved Home
Rule and, after careful consideration, on 20 September
1914 Redmond called on the Irish Volunteers to enlist in
the British Army. As there were Volunteer associations all
over Kerry, Ballymullen Barracks was expected to have
been overrun with would-be recruits. Although there
were posters and advertisements in the press, there were
no recruiting rallies in August or September. However, in
what they saw as an early blow against Britain, Republicans
on the Dingle Peninsula attempted to derail a train.

In Kerry, like the rest of the country, people were slow
to recruit as they waited for Redmond to decide whether
or not to support the war effort. Captain Godrey Drage,
who was posted to Tralee, was so disillusioned by the
slow recruiting that he went to England and recruited
1,000 men for the 6th and 7th Munster Fusiliers. Money
was raised for the people of Belgium and their story of
occupation, fact or fiction, was published in the local
press. The Catholic Church supported the war effort
and Redmond, which encouraged recruitment during
the opening phase of the war. Those who supported
Redmond and Britain's war effort were amongst the first
to enlist, as shown in Table 10.

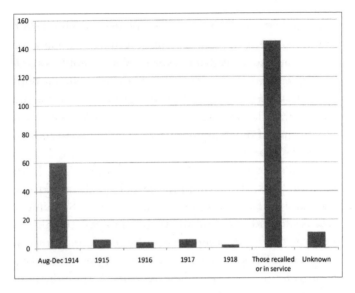

Table 10: Periods of enlistment.[72]

Recruiting in Ireland was not going to plan. The *Kerry Evening Post* reported that Kitchener was 'greatly disappointed with the poor response from the midlands and South of Ireland'.[73] Although the people of Kerry read about the exploits and destruction of the 2nd Munsters, they were not lining up to replace them. It was not until the middle of November that local MP Thomas O' Donnell returned to Tralee to aid recruitment. In Listowel a member of the Rural District Council and Board of Guardians was of the opinion that 'conscription in some form should be enforced'.[74] Another member of the board said that, 'while there is six and a half million of young Englishmen in England capturing the German trade that they should not ask Irishmen to go stop German bullets'.[75]

Soldiers' comfort funds were set up and many Belgian refugees arrived in South Kerry, no doubt with the help of some propaganda aided recruitment. The highlight of the recruiting campaign in January of 1915 was the send-off of four members of the RIC in Tralee as they left for the front. The article that carried the news also wrote, 'it is rumoured that some of the Volunteers who attended have expressed their desire to go to the front'.[76] In February 1915, Thomas O' Donnell returned to Tralee in an attempt to find more recruits. He announced to the crowd that, 'in the town of Tralee, 800 had joined the colours since the war began', and that, 'nearly 2,000 had joined the colours from this county'.[77] However the article does not actually mention the number of men who attended the meeting that joined the army.

A letter published in the *Kerry Evening Post* by an anonymous writer complained:

> In my district, comprising an area of 300 square miles, and many hundreds of men admirably suited for the war – not even as many as one man has joined the army since August 4th ... There have been various meetings for recruiting about here but the results have been very poor, rather different from meetings formerly in connection with National Volunteering.[78]

In April, the Band of the Irish Guards toured Kerry looking for recruits. On 17 April, they arrived in Tralee. A small recruiting office was established in Denny Street and all the local dignitaries were scheduled to speak. Again the reporting article concludes by talking about how successful the meeting was and how large the crowd that gathered was, but crucially, it does not report on the numbers actually recruited. A clue as to how successful the Irish Guards' tour of Kerry was advancing can be found in their Killarney meeting, where Sergeant Nicolson was reported to have said, 'I have come to the conclusion that the manhood of Ireland and England has absolutely gone to the dogs, and I consider it is near time the Government woke up and had conscription and make the wasters work for their living.'[79]

As the economic situation worsened and the threat of conscription grew, the citizens of Kerry looked to Eoin MacNeill and the Irish Volunteers. After the initial Volunteer split, the Irish Volunteers were going from strength to strength in Kerry. In their notes published in *The Kerryman* on 8 May 1915, they declared that all the national Volunteer organisations in Dingle, Camp and Killarney had, or were about to, declare for MacNeill. One week later Castlegregory and Firies declared for MacNeill, as rumours of an imminent conscription Bill were circulated in the press.

Despite increased support for MacNeill, recruiting was successful in some areas. The village of Clieveragh near Listowel contributed twenty-six out of a total of thirty males to the war effort. Successes like these were rare, but worse still for the recruiting sergeants was Eoin MacNeill's visit to Killarney on 24 May 1915. Special trains and bands travelled from throughout the county, where 1,500 Irish Volunteers were reviewed by MacNeill.

In June the Munster Fusiliers organised a recruiting tour of Kerry. At Cahirciveen a report of the meeting concluded that 'there was not a discordant voice at the meeting'.[80] Meanwhile, at the Kenmare leg of the Munsters tour, John Boland MP for East Kerry appealed for more men but a woman shouted out, 'the boys are wanted at home'.[81] Boland attempted to defend his record and proclaimed to

the crowd that he had 'represented them for fifteen years'.[82]
A voice from the crowd replied, 'Fifteen years too long.'[83]
At the Tralee leg of the tour it was announced that Tralee
'had sent twelve hundred men to the front'.[84] During the
meeting Timothy Houlihan was arrested and charged for
obstructing a recruiting meeting for shouting that, 'they
were all a pack of fools coming around here and preaching
the gospel'.[85] This was followed by clashes on the night of 15
June between Home Rule and Sinn Féin supporters. It was
clear even at this early stage that the people of Kerry were
not going to be supporting the war for too much longer;
there was an increase in people being arrested for violations
of the Defence of the Realm Act and support for Sinn Féin
was rising equally as fast. The Tralee Board of Guardians,
on 14 August, passed an anti-conscription resolution and
declared 'Sinn Féiners as good Irishmen as any'.[86]

Thomas O'Donnell warned farmers in October:

> Some people went around stating that if Germany conquered Ireland
> the farmers could tear up their land purchase agreements. That state-
> ment was incorrect in so far as that the purchase agreements would be
> torn up – not by the farmers – but by the agents of the Kaiser, into
> whose Exchequer they would be compelled to pay a crushing land tax.[87]

The following day a recruiting rally took place in Tralee but
no one had taken any take note of what O'Donnell had said.
The Kerryman reported, 'eloquent speeches were delivered,
but judging by the results they had not the desired effect as
we have not heard of any new recruits for the colours'.[88]

During November and December a further push
was made by the authorities for recruits. Throughout
November, the Band of the Royal Munster Fusiliers

travelled throughout the county, while in December, Lt Mike O' Leary V.C. toured Kerry. There was a change of tactics by the authorities at this point. They became sympathetic; in Abbeydorney the crowd were told the authorities were 'not asking for anything unreasonable. They could not expect men who were the sole support of their families or whose work at home was indispensable to go out, but there were plenty young men who could be spared.'[89] Despite this, a member of Tralee Board of Guardians wanted to send Thomas O' Donnell to Flanders and before he went to speak O' Donnell was heckled. A member asked, 'Why is he here at all?' Another replied, 'To earn his £400 a year.'[90] At the same time O' Donnell's fellow MP Michael Flavin was talking in Ballyduff with the intention of establishing a branch of the United Irish League. While he was speaking he was interrupted by a man who asked, 'What do you want coming here to get money for the league? Why don't you give £200 of your salary as a member?' Another remarked, 'What about the price of meal now?'[91]

The four Kerry MPs got themselves into further difficulty by not attending the annual meeting of the Irish Parliamentary Party in the Mansion House in February 1916. Sir Morgan O'Connell reported on recruiting in Kerry, 'Recruiting in this county, with a population of some 165,000, is dead. The open and avowed pro-German, anti-recruiting Sinn Féin element has been allowed to spread until every village in Kerry is rotten with it.'[92]

Although Kerry County Council passed a motion condemning the 1916 Rising, the writing was on the wall for recruiting in Kerry. In May 1916, Listowel Urban District Council passed a motion to aid the distress in Dublin in the aftermath of the Rising. There was a massive increase in Defence against the Realm Act violations and *The Kerryman* newspaper was suppressed in September. On 20 June 1917 the Kerrymen who had taken part in the 1916 Rising were released and returned to Tralee. During the jubilant scenes, bottles were thrown at wives of servicemen at the front. Although there was a rise in recruitment in 1917, it never equalled the levels achieved from August to December 1914. Once General Maxwell ordered the executions of the leaders of the Rising, he had at one stroke changed the course of Irish history.

His decision was the final straw for the people of Ireland. Many of them were struggling economically, and despite the sacrifices Irishmen made in British uniform it was to no avail. Kerry saw the 2nd Munsters wiped out at Etreux, they read of the disastrous landing of the 1st Munsters on V Beach at Gallipoli, and they also read of the appalling leadership shown by British Generals at Suvla. Yet the Government asked for more men. Where would these men be sacrificed and for what? The townspeople had given thousands of men, and why would farmers want to join the army? By 1916 the army had received all the men they were going to get and Maxwell had left Ireland with yet more Fenian dead. People did not know it at the time, but Ireland's future was decided in 1916.

BATTLE OF ETREUX

At the outbreak of the First World War, the 2nd Munsters were in training at Aldershot. They shipped out from Southampton on 13 August and arrived in Le Havre on the following day as part of the 1st Infantry Brigade. The Munsters left in good spirits; training had gone well and the battalion had just won the Connaught Obstacle Shield for the second successive year. They had beaten the 1st Battalion of the Coldstream Guards, who along with the 1st Battalion of the Scots Guards and the 1st Battalion of the Black Watch, made up the 1st Infantry Brigade. From 14-16 August the Munsters rested at Harfleur, before moving on to Le Nouvion on 17 August. On 22 August, the battalion began moving onto Bouey on the road to Mons. They marched toward Mons on a double march and passed within three miles of Etreux.

As the Munsters and the BEF advanced, the 5th French Army was attacked. The French, who had occupied the BEF's right flank, began to fall back, leaving the BEF exposed. This signalled the beginning of the retreat from Mons. On 24 August, the Munsters, along with the rest of the 1st Infantry Brigade, took up positions around Chapeau Rouge. The brigade was to cover the retreat of the BEF. It was here the Munsters had their baptism of fire. Major Charrier (the battalion's commander and a Kerryman) was under orders to hold the crossroads at Chapeau Rouge and told his men to dig in.

As the French withdrew, the 10th Reserve Army Corps of the German Army approached the positions held by the Munsters along two parallel routes. At 11a.m. the first German column attacked the Munsters dug in at Bergues and managed to capture the village. 'A' Company, defending the village, withdrew to the south. The second German column attacked 'B' and 'D' Companies of the Munsters who dug in around Chapeau Rouge. For one and a half hours the Germans attacked but could not break the well-entrenched defenders. During a break in the battle, the cooks of 'D' Company managed to bring up hot food.

The Germans now changed the focus of their attacks; having captured Bergues the only obstacle in their bid to surround the Munsters was 'C' Company in Femsy. The Germans, with their superior numbers, quickly captured the village. However, as the Munsters could now be surrounded easily, Captain Rawlinson of 'C' Company ordered a counterattack. The attack succeeded in driving the Germans back and the village was recaptured. The Germans now refocused their attention on Chapeau Rouge. Reinforced, they attacked once again using cattle as a shield in front of the men. Once again this attack failed and the Munsters began to withdraw toward the battalion headquarters outside of Femsy.

In Femsy, Major Charrier reorganised his order of battle for a retreat out of Femsy. 'B' Company was now on the right flank and 'D' Company to the left. The artillery preceded them to cover the withdrawal. All was going to plan until it was found that one section of 'D' Company had become engaged with the enemy. Once they were safely extracted the battalion resumed the march south toward

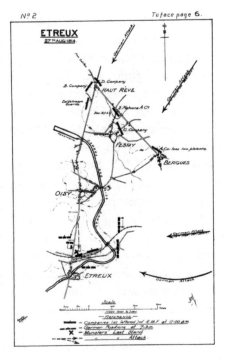

Original positions occupied by the 2nd Munsters.[94]

the village of Oisy. 'B' Company, on the right flank, was ordered to cover the retreat but became entangled with the Germans once more. They arrived in Oisy half an hour later than the rest of the battalion. This delay proved to be fatal, as the French on the right of the 1st Infantry Brigade had already pulled back, leaving their entire right flank exposed. Orders were issued to the 1st Infantry Brigade to retreat but the Munsters did not receive them as they were fighting to the north and east of the other elements of the brigade.

In Oisy, the Munsters realised they were on their own.

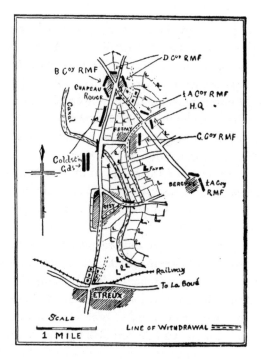

Map of the Munsters' retreat toward Oisy and Etreux.[95]

They continued to retreat in order to catch up with the rest of the Brigade. The battalion was to retreat south toward Etreux with 'C' Company, this time covering the retreat. Oisy stands just west of the Sambre–Oise Canal and had only one bridge with which one could cross into the village. This did not stop the Germans from attacking once again. On noticing the Munsters withdrawing, they attacked headlong over the bridge. This was easy meat for the Munsters, a regular professional battalion who held all the advantages against a force of German reservists.

The Munsters now held a strong position; however, the right column of the German 10th Reserve Army Corps was making for the town of Guise, twelve miles to the Munsters' rear. They passed within two miles of the fighting at Femsy and the Munsters retreated toward Oisy and stopped. It was this hesitation that let the other elements of the 1st Infantry Brigade retreat five miles south of Etreux, on the road to Guise. Major Charrier, noticing the Germans sudden halt, and hearing rifle and artillery fire to the north, mistook it for a British counterattack. Captain Jervis later wrote in *The 2nd Munsters in France*, 'Rumours of a big British counterattack were rife. Was this it?'[93]

Charrier believed it was, and ordered a halt to the retreat. Reconnaissance of the surrounding area was also ordered to figure out what was happening. The reconnaissance units reported that there was evidence of heavy fighting in the locality and they brought back some wounded Munsters. These reports, along with the sound of fighting to the north, encouraged the Munsters to dig in and wait for the advancing British Army. Worryingly, however, one reconnaissance group encountered some units of the 6th Reserve Dragoons and informed them that the Germans were massing north of Oissy. Charrier now saw the whole picture; the Germans were preparing another attack. To his right the German units that were supposed to be marching toward Guise would soon restart their march. If they crossed the River Sambre at Etreux before the Munsters they would be surrounded.

The Munsters now restarted their retreat toward Etreux. The men were ordered to advance down the sunken ditches along the side of the road while the two machine guns of the battalion fired down the centre to act as cover. The skill of the machine gun crews led by Lt Chute, a Kerryman, is to be praised. Despite the remainder of the battalion passing within a few feet of the firing line not a single man was hit. Captain Jervis wrote in a letter sent to Lt Chute's wife after her husband had been killed:

> The Germans were crossing the front, and he never neglected an opportunity of delaying their advance. He withdrew from one position to another, all day forming an invaluable escort to the two filed guns we had attached to us.
>
> The withdrawal continued through a village, at about 5.30, and at the other side of it he came into action again, firing right down the road, on both edges of which Captain Rawlinson's company was withdrawing. Owing to the help of your husband's guns the company got safely through and rejoined the battalion.[96]

With the Munsters rear now safe, thanks to the efforts of the machine gunners of the battalion, it was a race to Etreux. At the head of the Munsters was 'B' Company and just outside the village they saw a group of men double across the road. They attacked and called on the Munsters' attached artillery to support them. However, as they raced into action a shell burst nearby and killed or wounded most of the gun crews. The Munsters were now surrounded and the only way to safety was through Etreux. The Germans had time to entrench themselves and used the buildings in the village as defensive positions. With the artillery out of action the only way to break through was an unsupported frontal attack.

Major Charrier organised the attack and led the charge himself against a loopholed house, but the attack failed. Desperately, 'C' Company, who had just arrived on the scene, threw themselves against the fortified position but their attack also failed. This left 'D' Company to defend the rear, but they were now under increasing fire from all directions. Yet another attack was launched against the loopholed house, but again it failed. However an officer, Lt Wise, made it to the house and began firing in the loophole until he was struck in the head. Charrier, who was wounded in the last attack, now gathered the remnants of the two companies for a final attack. Charrier led the assault once more, but was killed and again the Munsters were driven back. In a letter home R. W. Thomas described the battle:

We fought for two days and just as we thought it was all over we found that we were surrounded, and so a desperate battle began. I could not describe the horrors of it on paper but we were about three quarters of a battalion fighting six German battalions, and without any chance of relief.[97]

It was now the turn of Captain Jervis and 'D' Company to attempt to break through. Instead of attacking down the road toward the house, Jervis took his men through fields on the eastern side of the road. At first the Munsters succeeded and made it as far as a hedge in front of the railway line. There were pinned down by enemy fire; they fixed bayonets and charged. The attack failed and with it the last hope of getting out of Etreux. The Munsters fell back to an orchard just north of the railway line to make their last stand. Surrounded, they began to run out of ammunition and Lt Chute 'crossed the road to find another target to aim at. As he crossed he was shot in the right side of the thigh and fell dead'.[98] Soon after, the machine guns ran out of ammunition, and so too did the rest of the battalion.

At 9.15p.m. the remnants of the Munsters, some 240 men including wounded, surrendered. The Germans were shocked to find that what stood in their way was a small

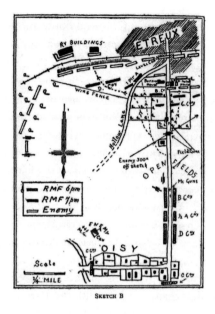

SKETCH B

Map of the Munsters' attempt to break through and their last stand outside Etreux.[99]

battalion. The main body of the British Army was now twelve miles from Etreux and the German Army was fourteen hours behind schedule. The *Kerry Evening Post* recorded that the Munsters lost '19 officers out of 23 killed or wounded, and 150 killed, and 200-300 wounded'.[100] It was a heavy price to pay, but five officers and 196 men did escape capture by evacuating with the Coldstream Guards earlier on 27 August. These men were mostly made up of the two platoons of 'A' Company who were not at Bergues at the beginning of the German attack on the battalion.

These platoons, along with reinforcements from the reserve battalions, went quickly back into the line to aid the 1st Infantry Brigade. Others from the Etreux action also had a lucky escape; Lance Corporal Forde and Private Lyon returned to Tralee on leave and told their story:

> They had been in action from 7.00a.m. till about 8.30p.m. and were worn out; they lost the other six comrades and found themselves alone in the morning. They did not know what direction to take but wandered around and lived on turnips for two days. They had several hair-breadth escapes. They went into a house where an old woman was alone. She took them to be Germans and was in trepidation … Afterwards they came very near a looting party of Germans, but eventually met a Frenchman who took them to a village where they met an old man who spoke English. They were cared for here, and escorted by relays to where a Captain of the Dublin Fusiliers was.[101]

The two surviving platoons of the Munsters took their place in the line again to cover with the 1st Infantry Brigade at the retreat from Charleroi. The retreat from Charleroi occurred in conjunction with the withdrawal from Mons. Again they were in the middle of the action, as this account from a Munster in Tralee on leave shows:

> The Germans turned up *en masse*. Their first few shells landed at our rear, but they soon found the proper range through their flying machines, which kept beyond our rifle range. We were digging our trenches when the first shells went wide, but before we had time to occupy the trenches the Germans got the accurate range. Our men withstood the fire bravely, though we were up against a regular stonewall of Germans. We mowed them down as we went through them, but as far as we went they were there still. After our thirty-mile march we were fairly worn out and besides the Germans were much better served with machine guns than we were.[102]

The German Uhlan Cavalry then surrounded the Munsters and captured two artillery pieces. The Munsters were ordered to recapture them and to break through the Uhlans. They did so in the form of a bayonet charge. Charlie Duggan from Boherbee in Tralee wrote of the attack:

> We might have surrendered, but that was our last hope, and when ordered to fix bayonets we gladly did so. There was an exciting tussle then for a while but we held the position. It was here I received my wound, but I never noticed it then. The Germans had abandoned some guns and with the joy of our success we dragged them back with us.[103]

The remaining Munsters had this time survived annihilation and retreated with the rest of the BEF. However they had once again lost heavily and after that action 'only 380 of the Munsters were left'.[104] In these early battles of the war the Munsters and indeed the BEF showed their strengths in leadership and general soldiering. In fact, the Battle Exploits Committee wrote of the Munsters in 1919:

> The action is likely to become the classical example of the performance of its functions by a rear-guard. The battalion not only held up the attack of a strong hostile force in its original position, thereby securing the unmolested withdrawal of its division, but in retiring drew on to itself the attacks of very superior numbers of the enemy. It was finally cut off at Etreux by five or six times its numbers, but held out for several hours, the remnant only surrendering when their ammunition was practically exhausted and only a small number of men remained unhurt. The survivors were warmly congratulated by the Germans on the fine fight they had made. No other claim to a memorial near Etreux is likely to be advanced – certainly nothing which would take second place to the Munsters.[105]

BATTLE OF RUE DU BOIS

After Etreux and the retreat from Mons, the 2nd Munsters were reinforced and given a new commanding officer in Lt Col. Bent. The battalion spent time in the rear, resting and training, before joining the 3rd Infantry Brigade. At the outbreak of the first battle of Ypres, the Munsters were ordered to hold positions around the Château of Hooge in Belgium. The Munsters, although fighting a peripheral role, fought for ninety-six hours before eventually being relieved. The 2nd Munsters, after fighting two defensive actions, then took to the offensive at Festubert on 22 December 1914. After marching for the most of thirty-six hours they arrived at Festubert at 4a.m. The Munsters orders were to attack at 7a.m., leaving them only three hours to rest and prepare for the attack. With no reconnaissance of the intended battlefield and poor artillery support, the Munsters attacked. In the first ten minutes of the attack, '11 officers and 200 men were hit'.[106] At 2p.m. the Munsters called on more artillery support so as to extricate themselves from no-man's land. However, the artillery landed their shells on the positions occupied by the battalion. Eventually, at 4a.m. on the following day, the Munsters managed to make their way back to their own trenches.

This is how the Munsters prepared for their first major attack of the war, at Rue Du Bois in northern France. The losses during the previous two battles had taken their toll and many of the regular soldiers had either been killed or wounded, 'Gaps had been filled again and again, and most of the Munsters who fought next day were newly come from Ireland and new to the life.'[107] The Munsters also had a new commanding officer in Col. Rickard.

The under-strength Munsters began 1915 with a period of quiet and reinforcement and team building. However, as Captain Jervis wrote:

When one writes of 'quiet' it must be remembered that it is a comparative term. There are many who prefer the stress of fighting to the eternal labour of building up and holding trench lines half under water, combining the worst form of amphibious warfare with training of the most intensive form … Everyday took its toll of the brave men – a stray shot here, an unlucky shell burst there, ever the watchful sniper ready to punish careless exposure whenever it occurred.[108]

Lt Creaghe-Harnett from Abbeyfeale on the Kerry–Limerick border wrote:

We live an awful life in the trenches, nearly always wet, and if you show your nose above the skyline you get a bullet either in or alongside it … As I am writing this in my 'dug out' shells are whistling and screaming overhead … and the German bullets keep hitting the top of the dug out.[109]

These front-line related fatalities combined with small attacks on the Munsters' position meant that the Munsters took many casualties. One of these small attacks took place on the Kaiser's birthday. A machine gunner in the battalion wrote:

On the morning of 25 January the Germans commenced a lively cannonade on the right and left of our positions as they were the weakest points in our line. Our batteries and heavy artillery soon began with deadly effect and lasted over three hours, smashing their trenches to a pulp. Shells were going at over 100 a minute – like hail stones. At about 8.30 the same morning large masses of Germans were to be seen advancing on the right of the canal which was about 50 yards across and it looked very critical for the time being. However we were not to be daunted, we held our ground until the last, but the numbers told. The battalion on our right had to fall back to their reserve trenches, leaving our battalion the Munsters in a terrible position and exposed to a murderous fire. Then came the most arduous task of the day, there was nothing for us but to retire from our brave Captain Hawkes. The next moment we heard our machine guns opening rapid fire at a rate of 500 rounds a minute covering our retirement; the machine guns were manned by Lieutenant Carrigan, Sergeant Walsh, M., and Lance Corporal Daly, E., both of Tralee.[110]

Sergeant Walsh went on to write:

We lost 3 killed and 97 wounded. We got off very lightly considering the heavy rifle and shell fire. We had to bring back 74 wounded Germans to the hospital to get dressed. They were Bavarians and Uhlans. I am specially mentioned in dispatches with L.C. Daly and Lieutenant Carrigan for holding our trenches for two hours with four machine guns while the company had to retire … I am expecting a French Military Medal for it.[111]

From January to May 1915 the battalion lost some 150 men and on 2 May the unit's strength was at 26 officers and nearly 700 men. This included Fr Gleeson as Chaplin for the battalion, who was held in high regard by the officers and men alike:

He did not believe in administering spiritual consolation in safety and comfort five miles behind the line. He brought the Holy Sacrament up to the firing line, and many a good Catholic of the Munsters has gone into battle fortified by Fr Gleeson's cheering words a few minutes before the action.[112]

In the aftermath of the Munsters' mauling at Festubert, the officers had learned some valuable lessons. At Festubert the Munsters had only three hours to prepare for the attack and this was seen as the main reason for its failure. For the Rue Du Bois attack, the practice was done on ground that resembled the ground at Rue Du Bois. Mobile prepared bridges would be used to cross a stream which flowed over the intended battlefield and aerial photographs of the German positions were handed out to officers. The attack planned for 'A' and 'B' Companies to attack first, followed by 'C' and 'D' Companies in support. The South Wales Borders and Gloucesters were in brigade reserve. To signify the capture of the Munsters' objectives, ten-foot poles, which were to be carried in the advance, would be erected upon their capture. To aid the advance, a forty-minute bombardment of the German trenches would precede the attack, followed by a creeping barrage to help cover the advancing soldiers.

On 8 May the Munsters arrived at Rue Du Bois and each company stood behind green flags with the word 'Munsters' embroidered upon them. It was then that Fr Gleeson gave the Munsters a General Absolution. The Absolution was captured in the painting by F. Mantania entitled *The Last Absolution of the Munsters at Rue Du Bois.*

At 5a.m. on the morning of 9 May (the attack was planned to take place on 8 May), the artillery barrage rained down on the German positions. After thirty-seven minutes

'A' and 'B' Companies climbed over the trenches, followed by 'C' and 'D' Companies. Unfortunately for 'B' Company a friendly shell wiped out an entire section. Although covered by a creeping barrage, the Germans began to fire upon the advancing Munsters. A strongpoint that had not been discovered in the planning stage began to take its toll on 'A' Company. According to the plan, when the Munsters were within fifty meters of the German lines, they were to lay down and await a second artillery bombardment to catch the Germans in the open.

Once the secondary barrage lifted, the Munsters made their way toward the German lines. 'A' and 'C' Companies could only manage to make their way to an area just in front of the German positions and were halted. 'B' Company, who had suffered heavily, managed to fight their way to the German trench and kill its occupants before continuing their advance. The orders of the battalion were to advance quickly, and the mopping up of the German trenches was to be conducted by another unit. However, as no other unit crossed the front line, 'B' Company became the focus of the German fire. They advanced to the stream and awaited the appearance of the bridges, which did not arrive. The stream offered 'B' Company some cover from the German fire. As the Germans began to retreat from their front-line trench, the river offered 'B' Company a strong position from which to fire upon them.

At this stage in the attack, it was clear that it had failed, and word was sent to the artillery to begin the attack again. They began to bombard the German trenches and rear areas, where 'B' Company was left in the open. They were all but wiped out except for two men who made it back to their starting positions. Lt-Col. Rickard now took command of the second attack but was killed just as it got underway.

The attack was again held up, and Major Gorham, now in charge of the battalion, ordered a withdrawal at 10.30a.m. At 11.00a.m. the Munsters lined up on the Rue Du Bois, only three officers and 200 men strong. The battalion lost nineteen officers and 370 men. Captain Jervis wrote:

> It is a remarkable fact that the attack, prepared with so much secrecy, was known in detail to the enemy, who inquired why it had been postponed! Added to this the complete inadequacy of the artillery preparation, an insufficient knowledge of the position to be assaulted, and the lack of co-operation between the various waves of the attack, and the failure of the assault can be understood.[113]

Major General Haking wrote after the action:

> I wish you also to convey to the CO 2nd Battalion Royal Munster Fusiliers my appreciation of the fine example set to the division by the successful assault of part of the leading line, a feat of arms which the Battalion must always be proud of, as this Battalion was the only one in the Brigade whose men succeeded in storming the enemy's breastworks.[114]

By the middle of 1915, the 2nd Battalion of the Royal Munster Fusiliers had lost most of the men who had been serving in the battalion in August 1914. The regulars of the BEF had quickly been killed or wounded, and the battalion had on three occasions since August 1914 been rebuilt. Was this down to poor leadership, poor tactics or maybe over-eagerness by some who put themselves in harm's way? What was clear was that after every action, the Munsters needed new soldiers. Were Kerrymen going to continue enlisting or would political events and disillusionment with the war make them think twice before taking the King's shilling?

GALLIPOLI: 'V' BEACH

When Russia declared war on Turkey on 5 November 1914, a new theatre of war was created. On 6 November Britain and France followed their ally's lead and declared war on Turkey. For Britain, any Turkish campaign would be a drain on her army's slim resources, although the Royal Navy saw it as an opportunity. The opening stages of the First World War were coming to a close, and stalemate set in during early 1915. It was clear to many military planners that the war could not be won in the West. Winston Churchill wrote:

> Shall we use our reinforced fleets and great new armies of 1915, either to turn the Teutonic right in the Baltic or their left in the Black Sea and the Balkans? Or shall we throw our manhood against sandbags, wire and concrete in frontal attack upon against the German fortified lines in France?[115]

Churchill's campaign for an attack on Gallipoli soon gained momentum and the navy were anxious to get underway. They committed fourteen battleships and two semi-dreadnoughts, but only one of these, the *Queen Elizabeth*, was a modern battleship. The French committed four battleships along with their support vessels. The fleet to attack the forts on the

Dardanelles was the largest ever to sail in the Mediterranean. Adding to the confidence of the commanders and crews would have been news of the success of the heavy German artillery had on the Belgian forts at Antwerp in 1914. However, the Turks and Germans had also made preparations for the expected attack on the Dardanelles. The Royal Navy had initially attacked the outer forts in November 1914 as the *Kerry Evening Post* reported, 'The bombardment of the Dardanelles yesterday morning lasted fifteen minutes when it ceased, but only momentarily. On being resumed it continued until ten o'clock. The bombardment was carried out principally by the English squadron, which threw several shells.'[116]

The Germans had reinforced the Turks with modern artillery, searchlights and more importantly, mines. On 25 February 1915, the naval attacks began on the straits. The attackers enjoyed initial success, destroying the outer defences at long range and forcing the infantry manning them to retreat. Marines were then put ashore on both sides of the straits, destroying gun emplacements, search lights, and other defences. Confidence was now so high that the military force that was expected to aid the navy would not be needed. Famously, in Chicago the price of wheat fell in the expectation of the straits being opened for the exportation of cheap Russian wheat. The *Kerry Evening Post* reported that, 'it is possible, therefore, that the opposition may be beaten down without the co-operation of a land force until a latter stage'.[117]

However, the Turks regrouped and drove the marines from the heights of Kum Kale at Cape Helles. The Turks now changed their tactics; they allowed the British to bombard them in the morning and let them pass further up the straits, before attacking them from behind in the afternoon. The attacks continued but were continually interrupted by poor weather. The second attempted landing of marines was driven back into the sea on 3 March. On 18 March the naval bombardment recommenced, but again the attack was foiled by mines and mobile batteries, as *The Kerryman* reported, 'Suddenly at 4.30p.m., from two places, just before Kephez Burnu appeared unexpected Turkish batteries one of 3 and one of 2 guns. From this place no fire had come all day, so they must have been movable batteries.'[118]

The Turks had also placed a new line of mines on the right side of the straits unknown to the British. These mines were placed at a point where the Turks knew the battleships would be turning. This new line of mines sunk the French battleship *Bouvet*, forced the abandonment of the *Ocean*, and damaged the *Irresistible*. The *Kerry Evening Post* concluded that:

> It seems therefore, that the operations of our navy in conjunction with the French have so far been more in the nature of a reconnaissance in force than the beginning of the grand attack. It has been necessary to determine precisely the nature of the resistance to be offered and, having done so, to await arrival of the large military contingents mustered to co-operate on shore.[119]

Even before the renewed attacks on 18 March, Kitchener had appointed General Sir Ian Hamilton as the man who would lead the amphibious invasion of the Gallipoli peninsula. On his appointment Hamilton wrote:

> My knowledge of the Dardanelles was nil; of the Turk nil; of the strength of our own forces next to nil. Although I have met K. [Kitchener] almost every day during the past six months, and although he has twice hinted I might be sent to Salonika; never once, to the best of my recollection, had he mentioned the word Dardanelles.[120]

After his appointment, Hamilton went about gathering intelligence and finding out what size of a force he would be commanding:

> Braithwaite set to work in the Intelligence Branch at once. But beyond the ordinary text books those pigeon holes were drawn blank. The Dardanelles and Bosphorus might be in the moon for all the military information I have got to go upon. One text book and one book of travellers' tales don't take long to master and I have not been so free from work or preoccupation since the war started. There is no use trying to make plans unless there is some sort of material, political, naval, military or geographical to work upon.[121]

Kitchener informed him that he would be commanding the inexperienced and unknown ANZAC forces of about 30,000 men and the 29th Division, whose strength was about 19,000 men, of which the 1st Battalion of Munsters were a part. There would also be the Royal Navy Division (about 11,000 strong) and a French Division, making a total of 80,000 men under Hamilton's command. However, the 29th Division was only on loan and was to be returned at the first available moment. Kitchener still believed in a naval victory as Hamilton writes, "'Supposing,'" [Kitchener] said, "one submarine pops up opposite the town of Gallipoli and waves a Union Jack three times, the whole Turkish garrison on the Peninsula will take to their heels and make a bee line for Bulair.'"[122]

At the outbreak of the war, the 1st Battalion of the Royal Munster Fusiliers was scattered all over India and Burma. They were shipped back to England in January of 1915 to aid with the home defence but were then earmarked for the Gallipoli campaign by Kitchener. As part of the 29th

Division they were professional, experienced soldiers and would be the key element in the campaign. For this reason, any offensive would have to wait for their arrival, Churchill wrote, 'Before any serious undertaking is carried out in the Gallipoli Peninsula, all the British military forces detailed for the expedition should be assembled so that their full weight can be thrown in.'[123]

Even if Hamilton wanted to land a force without the 29th Division, he could not, as 'transports are so loaded (water carts in one ship; water cart horses in another; guns in one ship; limbers in another; entrenching tools anyhow) that they must be emptied and reloaded before we can land under fire'.[124] These problems were compounded by the fact that intelligence of the enemy's strength on the peninsula was unknown. Hamilton wrote in his diary that:

> [General] Paris's appreciation gives no very clear lead. 'The enemy is of strength unknown,' he says, 'but within striking distance there must be 250,000.' He also lays stress on the point that the enemy are expecting us – 'Surprise is now impossible' ….The difficulties are now increased a hundredfold … To land would be difficult enough if surprise was possible but hazardous in the extreme under present conditions.[125]

The British knew nothing of the strength of the Turks but the Turks could easily ascertain the strength of the invading forces. Hamilton complained in his diary that because Egypt was not involved in the conflict, the British could not censor the Egyptian press, who 'continue to publish full details of our actions and my only hope is that the Turks will not be able to believe in folly so incredible'.[126]

On 4 April, twenty-one days before the planned invasion of the peninsula, Hamilton writes in his diary:

I have not shells enough to cut through barbed wire with my field guns or howitzers. I say also, I should much like to have some hint as to my future supply of gun and rifle ammunition. The Naval Division has only 430 rounds per rifle and the 29th Division only 500 rounds which means running it fine.[127]

It is clear that the military authorities were attempting to land a force of 80,000 men on the cheap. This force, had they been properly led and equipped, could have in fact captured the peninsula rapidly and marched on towards Constantinople. Churchill made reference to this in his multi-volume work on the First World War:

We now know that the force actually in the peninsula at this date was under 20,000, scattered along the coast in small parties without support or reserves. It seems probable that if the 29th Division had been on the spot in fighting order, it could have been landed, with whatever troops were sent from Egypt, at this period without severe loss, and could have occupied very important and probably decisive positions.[128]

This was the position the Allied forces found themselves in on the eve of what was at the time the largest amphibious invasion in history. The only comparison that can be drawn with the Gallipoli invasion is the D-Day invasion in 1944. The D-Day planners thought through every aspect of the landings and their aftermath; Hamilton didn't even know if the peninsula had wells. Alan Moorehead noted:

Men were sent into the bazaars of Alexandria and Cairo to buy skins, oil drums, kerosene tins – anything that would hold water. Others bought tugs and lighters on the docks; others again rounded up don-

keys and their native drivers and put them into the army. There were
no periscopes (for trench fighting), no hand grenades and trench-mor-
tars; ordinance workshops set to work to design and make them. In the
absence of maps staff officers scoured the shops for guide-books.[129]

On 24 April 1914, the orders were given to embark; the 1st
Battalion of the Royal Munster Fusiliers boarded the *River
Clyde* destined for 'V' Beach at Sedd el Bahr. The *River
Clyde* was a converted steamer with sally ports cut in the
sides. The men were to leave the ship via these sally ports
and run down gangplanks, before running across two lighters attached to the ship's bows to get to the shore. Inside the
River Clyde were 2,000 men, the entire 1st Battalion of the
Royal Munster Fusiliers, and those of the Dublin Fusiliers
and Hampshire Regiment who would not be landing with
their comrades on small craft, which would land prior to
the *River Clyde*.

At 5a.m. on 25 April, the battleship *Albion* opened up
on the village of Sedd el Bahr and 'V' Beach. The area was
known to have been reinforced and sown with barbed wire;
it was hoped the bombardment would destroy the wire
and remove the Turkish soldiers. After one hour of con-
stant bombardment without reply, it was judged safe for a
landing to take place. At 6.25a.m. the *River Clyde* beached
herself as planned, and the boats carrying the Royal Dublin
Fusiliers and Hampshire Regiment rushed forward towards
the beach. The Turks who were believed to have either fled
or been killed in their trenches, simply withdrew before the
bombardment and reoccupied their positions before the
landings. The Dublins and the Hampshires were met with
a hail of fire in their open boats. Some managed to struggle ashore, some were killed before they reached the shore,

while others clambered over the sides of the boats and drowned as they were weighed down by their sixty-pound packs. T.J. Lane, from Abbeyfeale on the Kerry–Limerick border, in a letter home wrote, 'The battle started at daybreak. The bombardment was simply hell let loose. It was one terrific din, with bursting shot and shell. The Turks were well entrenched and some of our brave Irish soldiers met their doom before they set foot on land at all.'[130]

The Munsters inside the *River Clyde* could hear the carnage outside and awaited their turn to attack. As they waited, Commander Unwin of the Royal Navy attempted to tie the lighters together to create a bridge to the shore. He did so in the face of heavy fire and strong currents, and then signalled for the Munsters to storm ashore. An unknown Munster Fusilier from Tralee wrote an account of the landing in a letter to a friend:

My Captain (Geddes) asked if we had platoons ready; I said yes; he shouted 'come on' he ran down the gangway, I after him; just as he got where the two gangways meet he got hit and fell into the water (the water was about ten feet deep); he shouted a few times so I thought he was gone. My God! Eugene! I cannot possibly describe how things went. Nearly everyone who got down the gangways was either killed or wounded. Well I got onto the other barge all right; fellows were falling all around; to hear them shouting 'mother, mother', 'father, father'! One poor fellow got hit through the forehead, he fell across my body; he started kicking on the deck and shouted for his mother twice. Then he shut up, I had to pull him off me, of course he was dead. In this boat there were about twenty killed and we could not see any of the snipers, as they were buried in the ground, I should say not 200 yards from us, so you could imagine at 200 yards a man is a good target. Then we had to jump overboard and wade waist deep in water.

Such a pelting we got! I saw one fellow in the water and about twenty bullets fell around him, but he got off alright until he reached the bank where he got one in the head. We then made a slight advance along the shore, there were about fifty yards of the bank barbed wired so we could not get any chance of cutting it.[131]

Another unknown Munster from Tralee wrote how some managed to make it to the beach:

Gangways had been thrown out on each side of the ship, but the moment the *Clyde* grounded shrapnel destroyed one of the gangways, leaving only one for the men to leave the ship by. The men had to run down a gangway as fast as possible, and take refuge in a barge until such time as the fire permitted their racing across a couple of planks to another barge, then to small boats, and so to the beach. Machine guns swept round continuously, and directly a man attempted to emerge on to the gangway he was picked off.[132]

The young soldier who believed Captain Geddes had been killed was mistaken. Myles Dungan, quoting from the Captain's memoir, has Geddes being hit, falling into the water but making it to the beach to command the survivors. The lighters forming the bridge to the shore came lose time and time again. This meant the Turks could focus their fire on the survivors huddled on the beach until the lighters were once more put back into positions for another attack. Eventually Col. Tizzard on board the *Clyde* decided not to continue landing men in daylight. The landing had been a disaster. Hamilton believed that 'Sedd el Bahr was supposed to be the softest landing of the lot, as it was the best harbour and seemed to lie specially at the mercy of the big guns of the Fleet'.[133]

The big guns of the fleet were at least supposed to clear the wire, and at best intimidate the Turkish soldiers into surrendering or leaving their posts. The bombardment failed to do either and the Turks occupied positions that were 'well entrenched and protected by three lines of barbed wire'.[134] The only thing protecting the troops on the beach was the *River Clyde*, whose 'own double battery of machine guns mounted in a sandbag revetment in her bows are to some extent forcing the enemy to keep their heads down and preventing them from actually rushing the little party of our men who are crouching behind the sandbank'.[135] It must also be noted that this was the very beach that the marines had landed on successfully the previous March.

Nightfall gave the troops on the beach a chance to regroup and for those still on board the *River Clyde*, a chance to disembark. They would, however, have to reorganise very quickly, as Turkish Commander Von Sanders would use the darkness as an opportunity to drive the troops on 'V' Beach into the sea. The senior officer on the beach was Major Jarret, who had the men take up an outpost line. A soldier from Kerry wrote home to say:

> I had just put out my sentry groups and Jarret came up to have a look when he was shot through the throat by my side. He died very soon, and left me the senior officer on shore. We had an awful night, soaked to the skin, bitterly cold and wet, and sniped at all night.[136]

In fact, that night, the Turks attempted six times to drive the Allies off 'V' Beach, and one soldier writing home claimed the Turks, 'captured some of the Dublins, tied them together and burned them. They cut the legs off some of ours'.[137] Although these accusations were never proven, it does show that there was a certain level of animosity between the Irish and Turkish soldiers.

On the morning of the twenty-sixth, the Munsters remained in a very dangerous position. The Turkish troops still held the key positions around 'V' Beach and the Munsters were in need of help. Attempts were made from 'X' and 'Y' Beaches, left and right of the Munsters respectively, to outflank the Turks at 'V' Beach. Both attacks failed, and the situation at 'Y' had gone so badly that by 12.20, an evacuation was well under way. At 7a.m. the remnants of Munsters, Dublins and Hampshires, began their attack on the medieval fortress of Sedd el Bahr. The fortress was located on the right side of 'V' Beach and contained up to 200 Turkish soldiers. The *Kerry Evening Post* records the battle:

> Then the command was given to take the fort. The heavy guns of the fort had of course, been silenced by the fleet, but it was holding about 200 of the enemy, with machine guns. Major Grimshaw of the Dublins, was now making himself very conspicuous, moving about courageously in the open, and rallying his men together. The Dublins, with the Munsters on their left, and the Hants on their right, assaulted the fort ... Before taking the fort the British had to retire owing to the British warships shelling the fort.[138]

After capturing the fort, the survivors of the three battalions attacked the village behind it. From the village of Sedd el Bahr, the Munsters came under fire from snipers with 'several weeks' provisions at their disposal'.[139] However, Private Moriarty, in a letter published in the *Kerry Evening Post*, wrote a description of the taking of the trenches from which the Turks had fired on the Munsters the previous day,

'We gave the enemy lead and steel and no matter of mercy either. You would be surprised to know the number of Germans with them, and when we charged their trenches they put up their hands and cried for mercy, but they got it with bullets and steel.'[140]

The Munsters had achieved the impossible; their planned landing had gone wrong from its inception. Hamilton and his fellow commanders had completely underestimated the strength and willingness of the Turkish soldiers to defend their homeland. Kitchener had forbidden Hamilton to fight in Asia, so the landings could effectively only take place in one place. The Turkish Army on the peninsula had been modernised since defeats in the Balkan Wars and its disastrous campaign against Russia. They knew the approximate strength of the Allies due to Egyptian press reports. They knew that a landing could only take place on the tip of the peninsula as the inner forts had not been destroyed. The Turkish troops were also given a massive morale boost when in March they had forced the unconquerable Royal Navy back out into the Mediterranean. The Munsters had to run down two gangways, one of which collapsed, across two lighters and wade to the beach. The plan was perfect if the landing had been uncontested, as the *River Clyde* would have emptied rapidly. Instead, the Munsters were slaughtered, with 'about 700 or 800 men either killed, wounded or drowned'.[141] There was a complete breakdown in communication from Hamilton to his subordinates, despite the fact that by his own admission he was very accessible:

Never, since modern battles were invented by the Devil, has a Commander-in-Chief been so accessible to a message or an appeal from any part of the force. Each theatre has its outfit of signallers, wireless, etc., and I can either answer within five minutes, or send help, or rush myself upon the scene at 25 miles an hour with the Q.E.'s fifteen inchers in my pocket.[142]

Hamilton was notified of the capture of the fort at Sedd el Bahr by Jack Churchill in the crow's nest of the *Queen Elizabeth*, but he then ordered the troops to withdraw from the fort in order for it to be shelled. The troops at 'Y' Beach on the right of 'V' Beach enjoyed an uncontested landing, yet Hamilton did not order them to advance and outflank the enemy at 'V' Beach until the following day. Hamilton watched the landings on 'V' Beach from the *Queen Elizabeth* but did not intervene as he did not want to interfere with the plans of Hunter-Weston (the commander of the 29th Division):

> Roger Keyes started the notion that these troops might well be diverted to 'Y' where they could land unopposed and whence they might be able to help their advance guard at 'V' more effectively than by direct reinforcement if they threatened to cut the Turkish line of retreat from Sedd el Bahr. Braithwaite was rather dubious from the orthodox General Staff point of view as to whether it was sound for G.H.Q. to barge into Hunter-Weston's plans, seeing he was executive Commander of the whole of this southern invasion. But to me the idea seemed simple common sense. If it did not suit Hunter-Weston's book, he had only to say so. Certainly Hunter-Weston was in closer touch with all these landings than we were; it was not for me to force his hands.[143]

Eventually Hamilton wired Hunter-Weston at 9.15a.m., asking him if he would consider landing more troops at 'Y' beach, to outflank the Turkish positions. Hamilton did not get a reply until 11.00a.m. Indeed the 29th Division was the elite outfit of the campaign, but Hamilton, on the first day, lost three of its battalions. The Munsters and Dublins were amalgamated to form the Dubsters, but only took the part of a reserve unit for the rest of the campaign until the amphibious landings at Suvla Bay. The story of 'V' Beach was truly a case of lions led by donkeys.

GALLIPOLI: SUVLA BAY

On 8 June 1915, General Sir Ian Hamilton received news that he would be receiving three divisions of the new army. One of the divisions he was about to receive was the 10th (Irish) Division under the command of Lt-Gen. Sir Bryan Mahon from Galway. Mahon, however, was not rated by Hamilton, who wrote, 'he is good up to a point and brave, but not up to running a Corps out here'.[144] The division was established almost immediately after the declaration of war, when Kitchener called on 100,000 men to form the first of the new armies. In Kerry, the call to arms was received and many Kerrymen joined the 6th and 7th Battalions of the Royal Munster Fusiliers. The 6th and 7th Munsters made up half of the 30th Brigade, along with the 6th and 7th Battalions of the Royal Dublin Fusiliers.

The 10th Division, like most other things earmarked for Gallipoli, was destined for calamity. Upon the creation of the new armies there was a huge demand for officers. This led to a situation where the War Office passed a rule where the Commanding Officer of a battalion could promote any promising recruit or experienced soldier. This, however, would lead to problems down the line as many had no military training whatsoever, save what they picked up at initial instruction. Other problems existed with the training, as Major Bryan Cooper recalls:

> The Infantry soon obtained rifles (of different marks it is true) and bayonets, but the gunners were greatly handicapped by the fact that the bulk of their preliminary training had to be done with very few horses and hardly any guns. Deficiencies were supplied by models, dummies and good will.[145]

At the end of April 1915, the 10th Division embarked for Aldershot for further advanced training. During this period, the 6th and 7th Munsters would have read with horror about the landing of the 1st Munsters on 'V' Beach. The King inspected the Irish soldiers on 28 May and on 5 July embarkation of the division began. It is worth noting at this point that the 30th Brigade, which included the two battalions of Munsters, embarked for Gallipoli without their artillery. This was going to create enormous difficulties for the Munsters and increase their casualties.

While the Munsters were training in Ireland, the situation in Gallipoli was going from bad to worse. At the ANZAC beachhead the soldiers only had six mortars and the artillery was being rationed to seventeen shells per day. Hamilton, too, was worried about the secrecy of any future large-scale operations on the peninsula, 'It is vitally important that future developments should be kept absolutely secret. I mention this because, although the date of our original landing was known to hardly anyone here before the ships sailed, the date was cabled to the Turks from Vienna.'[146]

Secrecy and surprise were to be the key of any new attack. After the disaster of the initial assault and the complete disregard for secrecy, Hamilton wrote that 'secrecy is so ultra-vital that we are bound to keep the thing within a tiny circle'.[147] However, on 24 June, only forty-three days before the landings on 6 August, Hamilton still did not know the landing site locations. He also, apart from Mahon, who we have already seen Hamilton did not rate, was still negotiating with Kitchener about what generals would command the various divisions and brigades. He wrote about Ewart and Stopford:

> With regard to Ewart. I greatly admire his character, but he positively could not have made his way along the fire trenches I inspected yesterday. He has never approached troops for fifteen years although I have often implored him, as a friend, to do so. Would not Stopford be preferable to Ewart, even though he does not possess the latter's calm?[148]

Kitchener, in a cable to Hamilton, wrote of General Hammersley, 'he will have to be watched to see that the strain of trench warfare is not too much for him'.[149] Hamilton then described Hamersley's appointment as commander of the 11th Division as 'ominous'.[150] For a finish, Hamilton had to settle for a combination of Stopford and Reed, of whom Hamilton wrote, 'the combination of Stopford and Reed is not good; not for this sort of job'.[151] This is where the confusion over the command begins; Stopford was in overall command, with General Reed his chief staff officer. The area around Suvla Bay was under the command of General Hammersley, who was in command of the 11th Division. His area of command also encompassed the 30th Brigade of the 10th Division, which was under the command of General Mahon.

While the high-ranking wrangling was going on, the

Munsters, along with the rest of the 10th Division, landed on the island of Mudros. It was here the men became acclimatised. The dust and flies played havoc with their food and they had to get used to water rations. Dysentery spread through the ranks and since there was a small Turkish minority living on the island secrecy was paramount. The troops, therefore, had no idea where they were going until they were briefed on board the ships taking them to Suvla Bay on 6 August. In fact, the operation had begun two days earlier, when some units landed on ANZAC to reinforce the Australians before the main attack. This was Hamilton's second large-scale amphibious operation of the campaign and he seemed to have learned the lessons from the 'V' Beach disaster. Intelligence units and Hamilton himself checked out the Suvla Bay area and found scarcely any opposition. On 25 April, Hamilton wrote in his diary, 'No sign of life anywhere, not even a trickle of smoke. The whole of the Suvla Bay area looks peaceful and deserted. God grant that it may remain so until we come along and make it the other thing.'[152] He went on to write:

> Suvla Bay should be an easy base to seize as it is weakly held and unentrenched whilst, tactically, any troops landed there will, by a very short advance, be able to make Birdwood's mind easy about his left. Altogether, the plan seems to me simple in outline, and sound in principle.[153]

Aerial reconnaissance then informed him that 'Suvla Bay is unentrenched, weakly held and quiescent, only yesterday a division of the enemy was reputed to be busy along the whole of the coastline to the south of Besika Bay.'[154] Crucially, however, the navy did not possess any charts of the proposed landing area in Suvla Bay. This was to have dire consequences for the landings. The day before the landings were due to take place, intelligence informed Hamilton that the Suvla Bay area contained, 'Not more than 100 to 150 yards of trenches in all; half a dozen gun emplacements and, the attached report adds, no Turks anywhere on the move.'[155] The plan for the Munsters was to land on 'A' Beach of the crescent-shaped Suvla Bay and capture Kiretch Tepe. The whole plan relied on speed, secrecy and surprise. Stopford had secrecy and surprise on his side and the plan relied on him pushing on out from the beachhead and capturing the heights behind.

At 9.30p.m. on 6 August, the navy put the men ashore at 'A', 'B' and 'C' Beaches. However, at 'A' Beach the navy's fears were realised when many of the new landing craft were caught on the reefs and the men had to wade to shore. Because of these difficulties, the navy decided to land the Munsters further north at 9.00a.m. on 7 August. Matthew Broderick from Clonmel wrote home:

We were put into a lighter, but the enemy's artillery fire was too heavy where we were to land, and we had to remain where we were until the naval guns silenced their artillery. Then all pushed towards the shore until we got to within 40 yards of it, as the lighter could not get any closer. Then we had to jump into the water. Some were swimming, more making their way as best they could, holding their rifles above their heads. To our great surprise, the men who got on shore first were completely blown up by concealed land mines, and that had a terrible effect on the rest of us, as we were making our way ashore. But in spite of all difficulties we succeeded in landing, and then we quickly formed up and started to advance. We had not got far when we came under fire. Nevertheless, we kept advancing and after covering some hundreds of yards we came closer to the to the Turks' fire.[156]

This advance was the single largest advance of the day among all the invasion beaches. Stopford had successfully landed troops on every beach and unlike the April landings, once the Allies were ashore they established themselves. However, Stopford never told his men to push on and so never captured their objectives. Stopford was not even in contact with Mahon and the 30th Brigade, so when Hamilton landed he had to find Mahon himself. When Hamilton found Mahon, he found chaos; Mahon was in command of some of Hammersley's men and Hammersley in charge of some of Mahon's. However Mahon was making progress up Kiretch Tepe, his main objective, and Hamilton was willing to let him be. This was Hamilton's main weakness; he did not seem to be able to force himself or his ideas upon his subordinates. In his diary he writes:

> My own idea would certainly have been to knock the Turks out by a bayonet charge – right there. So far they had not had time to dig a regular trench, only a few shallow scrapings along a natural fold of the ground. If Mahon wished to make a turning movement, then, I think, he would have been well advised to take it by the north where the ground over which he must advance was not only unentrenched and clear of brush, but also laid quite open to the supporting fire of the Fleet. But I kept these views to myself until I could see Stopford.[157]

The forces on Kiretch Tepe never captured the full length of the ridge, and that was their chance. It would have been risky, but Hamilton had made the same mistake in April by not forcing Hunter-Weston to outflank 'V' Beach, from 'X' and 'Y' Beaches. Stopford, unlike Hamilton, knew what he wanted, however this was to take all the momentum out of the Munsters' attack. At 7.00a.m. on the morning of 8 August, he ordered Mahon to dig in on Kiretch Tepe. On the twelfth Mahon launched an unauthorised attack on the Turkish trenches in front of him at Kiretch Tepe and captured them. Things got so bad that on 15 August, nine days into the battle, Hamilton sacked Stopford and replaced him with General de Lisle. On the same day the Munsters launched another attack on Kidney Ridge, but it was to fail. Worse still, Mahon had taken de Lisle's promotion as an insult. Mahon was his senior, but Hamilton felt he would be more valuable as the commander of the 10th Division. General Mahon therefore resigned mid-battle and the whole Suvla Bay landings became a catastrophe. An unknown Kerryman in the Munsters wrote home describing the battle for Kidney Ridge:

> The Turkish shells from their small guns are not much use, they merely make you duck when you hear them, but some of their big guns are good value. All vegetation is scorched up, one meets hollyhocks, and all sorts of thorny scrubs and undergrowth all dried up. The Turks have fired this several times and in one place a lot of theirs and our wounded got burned up.[158]

The level of censorship around the Suvla campaign was immense, making it very difficult to find primary accounts in the local press. The Munsters were forced to advance up a 700-metre hill without their artillery support. Instead they were relying on those manning the ships in the bay who really did not know what they were firing at. The 30th Brigade could have easily have captured Kiretch Tepe but Stopford ordered them to dig in on the morning of 8 August. On 15 August things came to a head for Mahon and he resigned during the battle for Kidney Ridge. This left the Munsters leaderless and relying on their untrained junior officers. If the April landings were a disaster, then the Suvla landings were an embarrassment – no wonder the authorities involved with censorship kept the lid on the whole episode. Major Bryan Cooper later wrote, 'The 10th Division had been shattered; the work of a year had been destroyed in a week, and nothing material had been gained.'[159] To add insult to injury the Allies gained little or no more ground from the end of August until they withdrew on 8 January 1916.

After the Suvla landings another two battalions had to be rebuilt. Events in Ireland were moving at pace and therefore it was far more difficult for the authorities to raise the reinforcements needed, reinforcements that even before the campaign were hard to come by. As Hamilton notes of the 10th Division before the Suvla landings, 'not more than 60 per cent of the men are Irish, the rest being either North of England Miners or from Somerset'.[160] Many of these men had given their lives in the belief they were fighting for Ireland, but the 1916 Rising had changed the Irish political landscape forever. Thoughts these men had of returning to Ireland as conquering heroes must have all but evaporated.

CONCLUSION

Shortly after the Great War in Europe finished in November 1918, the Irish War of Independence began on 21 January 1919. The lessons of 1916 had been learned and the ideals of the Rebellion's leaders were firmly engrained in the minds of the members of the IRA. Those who returned from the trenches found themselves amid another conflict. These demobilised soldiers were probably shocked to find themselves in a completely new Ireland. The heroes were the Volunteers and Sinn Féin, not the former soldiers and the Irish Party.

On 11 November 1924, the first Armistice Day ceremony took place in Tralee. Five hundred ex-servicemen took part in a procession, which began at Day Place and moved onto St John's Catholic church on Castle Street where Mass was celebrated. The Protestant ex-servicemen marched onto Nelson Street (now Ashe Street) for a ceremony at St John's Protestant church. After the ceremonies, the procession moved onto Rath Cemetery where wreaths were laid on the graves of dead soldiers. *The Liberator* reported that the parade was 'watched by big concourses of people *en route*'.[161] The parade was led throughout the day by the children of dead servicemen wearing their fathers' medals, and music was provided by the British Legion's Fife and Drum band. This was to become the route and the form that all Armistice Day parades would take until 1938.

The seventh anniversary of the Armistice in 1925 was celebrated by 400 ex-servicemen, 100 short on the previous year. Major MacGillycuddy stated that 'if they [The British Legion] had sufficient funds at their disposal the parade would have been much larger'.[162] The 1926 celebration proved to be the most controversial. The parade itself passed off peacefully, unlike others in Limerick and Dublin, but it was a Tralee Urban District Council (UDC) meeting that proved to be controversial. Tom Dennehy, Chairman of the UDC, informed the council that he 'thought we were rid of these imperialistic bumkum displays in this town'.[163] John Joe Sheehy, whose brother died during the war, also objected stating, 'nobody objected to these people commemorating the day, but when it sought to merge political propaganda into it he should object, after all these workmen were only dupes'.[164] John O' Leary, chairman of the Tralee branch of the British Legion, replied to the comments in a letter published in *The Kerry News*, 'I have also been informed that our loud speaking Tom, never fired a shot for the Irish Republic ... The hypocrisy of patriots of Tom Dennehy's calibre, has made poor Ireland what it is.'[165]

The debate between Dennehy and O'Leary continued throughout November but the attention of the ex-servicemen was more focused on the Irish Trustees for Housing British Ex-Soldiers and Sailors. By November 1926 they had purchased land in both Tralee and Listowel, while negotiations were ongoing in regard to purchasing land in Killarney. An article in *The Kerryman* complained that 'only for the attitude taken up by the last Tralee Urban District

Council when the matter came before them, it is not four-teen, but sixty houses would be built'.[166] At the following meeting between Tralee UDC and the housing trustees, a further two houses were negotiated. Sixteen houses for the ex-servicemen was simply not enough; as we have already seen that from the available service records, 163 men returned. This equates to only 9.8 per cent of the 163 ex-servicemen being granted a house.

The 1927 commemoration took the same route as previous years. Major MacGillycuddy, with the comments made by John Joe Sheehy and Tralee UDC in 1926 ingrained in his mind, informed the ex-servicemen in his speech that:

> They assembled for two purposes only, to commemorate the sacrifices made in the World War for civilisation, and secondly, by their presence to keep in memory the fact that a devastating war was not long passed, and by keeping this fact in mind they were proving that they were prepared to prevent another war.[167]

Like previous years, the event was well attended in Tralee. Nationally, ex-soldiers questioned how the Government would commemorate their dead comrades. Throughout March 1927 the new Irish Government debated where to locate a monument dedicated to the memory of the Irish Great War dead. On 29 March, the Dáil debated whether or not to locate the monument in Merrion Square. Kevin O'Higgins questioned locating a memorial opposite Leinster House:

> I say that any intelligent visitor, not particularly versed in the history of the country, would be entitled to conclude that the origins of this state were connected with the park and the memorial in that park, were

connected with the lives that were lost in the Great War in France, Belgium, Gallipoli and so on. That is not the position. This state has other origins, and because it has other origins I do not wish to see it suggested, in stone or otherwise, that it has those origins.[168]

O'Higgins did however go on to say:

I want it to be understood that I speak in no spirit of hostility to ex-servicemen, qua ex-servicemen. Two members of my family served throughout that war – one who did not survive, in the British Army, and another who did in the navy – and so it will be understood that it is no feeling of hostility to those who were through that war in the ranks of the British Army that I oppose this scheme.[169]

The tenth anniversary of the conclusion of the Great War was commemorated by approximately 300 ex-servicemen in Tralee,[170] while for the first time an article in the local press commented that 'the poppy was well displayed throughout the town'.[171] The 1929 parade had to be partially abandoned due to flooding, but the anniversary was also used by the Irish Trustees for Housing British Ex-Soldiers and Sailors to highlight the plight of ex-servicemen. They informed a meeting in Killester, County Dublin, that, 'under the Land Trust 2,626 houses were allotted to the Irish Free State for ex-servicemen and, although nearly ten years has elapsed, this number has not yet been provided'.[172] Prior to the Armistice Day commemoration in 1930, John O'Leary told a meeting of the Tralee Branch of the British Legion that, 'apparently the ex-servicemen of Tralee are asleep, because grants, benefits, etc., are continually coming into Listowel, Killarney, Killorglin, etc., whilst Tralee evidently deserves nothing'.[173] These comments came after O'Leary told the meeting that, 'Instances had occurred in Tralee where ex-servicemen's widows had to beg [around] the town to bury their husbands.'[174] The ceremony that year was observed in a similar manner to those of previous years, but for the first time the Protestants of Listowel held their own ceremony. This undoubtedly reduced the numbers taking part in the main events in Tralee.

Throughout the early 1930s, Remembrance Day parades took place in Tralee but were not well documented in the local press. It is impossible to know how many ex-servicemen attended the ceremonies, but on 13 November 1933, 2,000 people[175] attended the unveiling of a monument dedicated to Captain James Lawler, who was killed by Free State forces during the Civil War. The high turnout for the unveiling is in stark contrast to the declining numbers of people attending the Armistice Day commemorations, which by 1938 had declined to sixty ex-servicemen. The 1938 ceremony came one year after the British Legion's premises were broken into and ransacked.

It was also in 1938 that the National War Memorial was to be opened after much negotiation. It was the location of the memorial that was causing difficulty. The memorial was to be in Dublin, but where? Merrion Square could not be used as it may give the wrong impression to visitors. Trinity College could not be used as it would be seen as too pro-unionist. Parnell Square, where the Garden of Remembrance would later open 1966, was unsuitable as it was too close to the GPO. St Stephen's Green was already the location of an arch commemorating the Dublin Fusiliers who died in the Boer War. (The arch is also known as 'Traitors' Gate'.) Eventually, Senator Andrew Jameson suggested a twenty-acre site at Islandbridge. His suggestion was adopted by the War Memorial Committee in December 1931. The site was completed in January 1938 and was due to be officially opened by Taoiseach Éamon de Valera on 10 May 1939. However due to the worsening European situation, de Valera felt he could not open the memorial. It was therefore not officially opened until 1 July 2006 by President Mary McAleese and then then-Taoiseach Bertie Ahern. The period between May 1939 and July 2006 became an era of national amnesia. W.B. Yeats had predicted this in 1927. He said during the Seanad debate on locating a national memorial, 'Armistice Day will recede. These men will not live forever. I hope it is not going to become a permanent political demonstration in this country, to be carried on by the children of ex-servicemen. It will grow less and less each year.'[176]

To commemorate an event, we must fully understand what we are commemorating. The first question we must ask ourselves is why did these men enlist in the British Army? After the initial surge in recruitment from August to October 1914, enlistment began to drop off. There are many reasons for this slump. After Redmond gave his speech at Woodenbridge, County Wicklow, thousands of men enlisted in the belief they were fighting for Home Rule. These Home Rule supporters were amongst the first to enlist, along with adventure seekers, war romantics, and unionists. Kerry was no different from any other part of Ireland in this regard, but as Kerry was a largely a rural county, farmers who had been suffering from the foot and mouth crisis were now selling their products at record prices. This gave no reason for anybody involved in farming to enlist, but it gave every reason for those living in urban areas to enlist, as there was no money available for public work schemes. This, in essence, means that the majority of Kerrymen joined the army, not for patriotic reasons, but for economic reasons. By the end of 1915 the British Army had received the majority of men that were going to enlist voluntarily. This is also due to the fact that the majority of men who would have enlisted were already in uniform.

The quality of training must also be brought into question. As we have seen through Bryan Cooper's official history of the 10th (Irish) Division, the men trained with obsolete equipment and the junior officers lacked basic officer training. This is in no way the men's fault, but it gave them no chance in the cauldron that was Gallipoli. The new armies were in complete contrast to the well-organised, properly led, well-disciplined and professional pre-War units. These characteristics enabled the 2nd Munsters to make a stand at Etreux as well as allow the BEF to fight such a well-organised retreat from Mons. Indeed the losses incurred by the 1st, 6th and 7th Battalions of the Munsters at Gallipoli and the heavy losses the 2nd Battalion suffered in France, in no doubt affected recruiting.

The majority of men from Kerry took the King's Shilling because they had to do so. It is an unfortunate reality; although many did enlist for several other reasons, economics in my view was the main motive. This motive continues to this day – the *Irish Independent* recorded that:

> The British Army, in a statement, indicated that 10.5 per cent of enlistments in Northern Ireland were from the South. This compares with 4.5 per cent the previous year and 3 per cent in 2005/2006. The rise in recruits from the Republic was attributed by enlistment officers to economic conditions and in a change in attitude in the South toward a career in the British Army.[177]

For this reason, as well as the historical overlap that occurs between the Great War and the 1916 Rising, commemoration is difficult. Kevin O'Higgins's argument about the origins of the State are correct; although many thousands of Irishmen died in France and Gallipoli, the origins of the state are in the GPO. The question is: where do they belong in Irish history and what is their relationship with the men who took part in the 1916 Rising? The bravery of the Kerrymen who fought in France and Gallipoli and their place in history is not in question. The Island of Ireland Peace Tower at Messines in Belgium, where the 16th Irish Division and the 36th Ulster Division fought side by side, serves as a monument of reconciliation between unionists and nationalists. However, like the war, it's 'over there' and we are left with the same problem of how we recognise these men. R.F. Foster claims that 'The First World War should be seen as one of the most decisive events in modern Irish History.'[178] It is a decisive moment but not the seminal moment. Within the next decade we will be commemorating both the centenary of the 1916 Rising and the conclusion of the Great War. There is no doubt that at an academic and official level the memory of those killed in the First World War will be honoured. Will there be more than a glancing recognition at a public level? A national interest and debate must be created, not in the academic 'ivory tower' but in the public sphere. This can only be created by educating the public using all forms of the media.

Ex-servicemen from all backgrounds took part in commemorative events in Kerry until 1938. Since then, their story has largely been forgotten. Today's modern Ireland, after the ninetieth anniversary of the Easter Rising and the controversy surrounding the visit of the English Rugby

Team and the playing of 'God Save the Queen' in Croke Park, is ready for a national debate. A national debate may prove to be divisive, however Redmond's decision to support Britain was divisive, but put in motion a chain of events that led to the 1916 Rising and that was the War's biggest effect on Ireland.

APPENDIX 1

LIST OF KERRYMEN KILLED WHO WERE OFFICIALLY RECORDED.[179]

Name	Date of Death	Location of Death	Home Address
Adams, Joseph George	03/09/1916	France	Killarney, Co. Kerry
Ahern, John	07/07/1916	British Expeditionary Force	Tralee, Co. Kerry
Ashe, Francis	05/09/1915	France	Tralee, Co. Kerry
Baily, John	17/06/1916		Tralee, Co. Kerry
Barrett, Patrick	10/11/1917	France	Tralee, Co. Kerry
Barry, John	17/03/1917	France	Listowel, Co. Kerry
Barry, Michael	17/07/1917		Listowel, Co. Kerry
Bellingham, George	05/03/1918		Co. Kerry
Bennett, Alfred	26/04/1915	Gallipoli	Ballyseedy, Tralee, Co. Kerry
Blundell, William	24/04/1917	Salonika	Listowel, Co. Kerry
Boyle, Thomas	12/07/1915	Gallipoli	Listowel, Co. Kerry
Brennan, John	27/08/1914	France	Listowel, Co. Kerry
Broder, John	07/05/1915	Gallipoli	Listowel, Co. Kerry
Brooks, Harold	08/08/1915	Gallipoli	Killarney, Co. Kerry
Brosnan, John	12/11/1915	France	Castleisland, Co. Kerry

Browne, Michael	28/11/1916	France	Tralee, Co. Kerry
Bundy, Frederick	27/10/1914	France	Tralee, Co. Kerry
Burke, William	10/11/1917	France	Lisselton, Co. Kerry
Burns, Patrick	10/11/1917	France	Ballybeg, Sneem, Co. Kerr
Butler, Frederick William	20/09/1917	France	Tralee, Co. Kerry
Byrnes, William	02/05/1915	Gallipoli	Listowel, Co. Kerry
Cahill, Maurice	05/11/1915	France	Coolmagort, Co. Kerry
Canavan, James	10/10/1918		Listowel, Co. Kerry
Canty, Matthew	09/05/1915	France	Kilflynn, Co. Kerry
Carey, Daniel	06/11/1918		Killroglin, Co. Kerry
Carey, Patrick	17/11/1915	SS *Anglia*	Kilgarvan, Co. Kerry
Carmody, Edward	04/05/1917		Listowel, Co. Kerry
Carrol, Denis	09/05/1915	France	Listowel, Co. Kerry
Cherry, Bernard	09/05/1915	France	Tralee, Co. Kerry
Clifford, Timothy	25/08/1916	France	Killorglin, Co. Kerry
Coffey, Daniel	04/11/1917	Salonika	Tralee, Co. Kerry
Coffey, Michael J.	08/08/1918	France	St John's, Tralee, Co. Kerr
Coghlan, Charles	27/09/1918	France	Tralee, Co. Kerry
Colgan, Edmund	30/06/1915	Gallipoli	Tralee, Co. Kerry
Collins, Michael	22/03/1918	France	Ballylongford Co. Kerry
Connolly, Edward	05/07/1916	France	Tralee, Co. Kerry
Connor, Henry	18/07/1916	Egypt	Killorglin, Co. Kerry
Connor, Thomas	17/09/1914	France	Listowel, Co. Kerry
Connor, Timothy	29/08/1916	France	Tralee, Co. Kerry
Conroy, John	26/12/1916	Greek Macedonia	Tralee, Co. Kerry

Conway, Charles	09/09/1916	France	Tralee, Co. Kerry
Cooney, Michael	29/03/1918	France	Farranfore, Co. Kerry
Corcoran, Michael	09/05/1915	France	Cahirciveen, Co. Kerry
Courtney, Maurice	04/11/1916	France	Killarney, Co. Kerry
Cronin, Daniel	09/05/1915	France	Milltown, Co. Kerry
Cronin, Patrick	17/05/1916	France	Kilgolinet, Co. Kerry
Cronin, Timothy	30/03/1918	France	Tralee, Co. Kerry
Crowley, John	21/08/1916	France	Dromlough Co. Kerry
Cull, Michael	30/04/1915	France	Tralee, Co. Kerry
Culloty, Patrick	28/06/1918	France	Scartaglen, Co. Kerry
Curry, John	30/07/1916	France	Tralee, Co. Kerry
Curtayne, Richard	15/09/1916	France	Tralee, Co. Kerry
Dalton, Daniel	24/08/1914	France	Castleisland, Co. Kerry
Daly, Denis	09/05/1915	France	St John's, Tralee, Co. Kerry
Daly, Denis	26/12/1916		Listowel, Co. Kerry
Daly, Michael	02/01/1917		Cahirciveen, Co. Kerry
Dannaher, William	19/07/1917	France	Listowel, Co. Kerry
Day, Joseph	09/09/1916	France	Killarney, Co. Kerry
Dee, Michael	20/10/1918	France	Listowel, Co. Kerry
Dennehy, Daniel	05/10/1916	France	Dromid, Co. Kerry
Dennehy, Daniel	12/07/1916	France	Tralee, Co. Kerry
Dillon, Thomas	15/11/1914	France	Beale, Co. Kerry
Dinneen, William	21/04/1916	France	Lixnaw, Co. Kerry
Dodd, Robert	21/08/1915	Gallipoli	Killarney, Co. Kerry
Donnelly, Michael	19/07/1915	France	Tralee, Co. Kerry

Donoghue, Jeremiah	28/07/1916	France	Killorglin, Co. Kerry
Dooley, Thomas	10/10/1918		Tralee, Co. Kerry
Dore, John	13/02/1916		Tralee, Co. Kerry
Dore, Michael	08/10/1916	Greek Macedonia	Listowel, Co. Kerry
Dowd, Jeremiah	19/10/1914	France	Tralee, Co. Kerry
Downes, Maurice	23/03/1918	France	Listowel, Co. Kerry
Ducie, Joseph	27/08/1916	France	Tralee, Co. Kerry
Dudley, William	27/08/1916	France	Tralee, Co. Kerry
Dunford, Michael	24/01/1917	France	Duagh, Co. Kerry
Dwyer, Patrick	23/03/1915	France	Cahirciveen, Co. Kerry
Eagar, William George Massy (Billy)	21/08/1915	Suvla Bay	Co. Kerry
Egan, Alfred Henry	01/06/1918	France	Cahirciveen, Co.Kerry
Elligott, Patrick	09/06/1917		Tralee, Co. Kerry
Enright, John	29/09/1918	France	Listowel, Co. Kerry
Falvey, Denis	17/09/1916	France	Listowel, Co. Kerry
Fauchon, Robert	12/05/1917	France	Sluicetown, Co. Kerry
Fennell, James	27/08/1915	France	Tralee, Co. Kerry
Fenton, Maurice	28/02/1916	France	Dingle, Co. Kerry
Finn, Patrick	09/10/1917	France	Castlegregory, Co. Kerry
Finnegan, Timothy	04/10/1918	France	Kenmare, Co. Kerry
Finnerty, Jeremiah	27/08/1914	France	Tralee, Co. Kerry
Finnerty, John	21/12/1914	France	Tralee, Co. Kerry
Fitzgerald, Michael	09/05/1915	France	Tralee, Co. Kerry
Fitzgerald, Timothy	02/11/1916	France	Tralee, Co. Kerry
Fitzgerald, William	17/01/1917	France	Tralee, Co. Kerry

Fitzgibbon, Edward	11/02/1918		Tralee, Co. Kerry
Fitzmaurice, Maurice	12/11/1914	France	Duagh, Co. Kerry
Fitzmaurice, Thomas	27/08/1914	France	Lixnaw, Co. Kerry
Fitzmaurice, William	21/03/1918	France	Tralee, Co. Kerry
Fitzpatrick, Timothy	05/10/1918	France	Tralee, Co. Kerry
Flavin, Peter	03/06/1916	France	Tralee, Co. Kerry
Fleming, David	11/09/1917	France	Kilcummin, Co. Kerry
Fleming, Patrick C.	12/01/1917	France	Killarney, Co. Kerry
Flynn, Patrick	01/05/1915	Gallipoli	Killorglin, Co. Kerry
Foley, Patrick	21/03/1918	France	Glenbeigh, Co. Kerry
Foley, Richard Henry	16/08/1917	France	Listowel, Co. Kerry
Galvin, Timothy	17/01/1917	France	Brosna, Co. Kerry
Gibney, Bernard	09/04/1917	France	Listowel, Co. Kerry
Giles, Bertie John	08/07/1918	France	Gransha, Co. Kerry
Godfrey, Christopher	25/09/1917	Egypt	Listowel, Co. Kerry
Godfrey, James Andrew	03/05/1917	France	Killarney, Co. Kerry
Goodwin, William Alexander Delap	01/07/1916	Somme	Tralee, Co. Kerry
Grace, Christopher	17/08/1915	Gallipoli	Tralee, Co. Kerry
Grady, Denis	13/05/1915	France	Cahirciveen, Co. Kerry
Granville, John	01/07/1916	France	Tralee, Co. Kerry
Greaney, Thomas	27/08/1914	France	Listowel, Co. Kerry
Griffen, James	19/03/1915	France	Killorglin, Co. Kerry
Griffen, James	08/05/1917	France	Cahirciveen Co. Kerry
Griffen, John	01/10/1915	France	Killorglin, Co. Kerry
Griffen, Joseph	21/01/1916	Mesopotamia	Tralee, Co. Kerry

Guerin, Jerome	02/09/1916	France	Killarney, Co. Kerry
Guinane, John	07/09/1916	France	Tralee, Co. Kerry
Hallaron, Maurice	10/11/1917	France	Kenmare, Co. Kerry
Hanley, Timothy	08/03/1917	France	Kenmare, Co. Kerry
Hanon, Maurice	10/11/1917	France	Lixnaw, Co. Kerry
Hannon, John	22/03/1918	France	Muckross, Killarney, Co. Kerry
Harrington, Jeremiah	25/12/1914	France	Kenmare, Co. Kerry
Harrington, John	13/03/1916	France	Kenmare, Co. Kerry
Harrington, Michael	26/07/1917	France	Tuosist, Co. Kerry
Harris, Gerald Patrick	13/01/1918	France	Tarbert, Co. Kerry
Hayes, Michael	09/01/1916	France	Killarney, Co. Kerry
Healy, Dan	23/07/1918	France	Kilgarvan, Co. Kerry
Healy, Daniel John	21/10/1914	France	Tralee, Co. Kerry
Healy, Martin	09/09/1916	France	Ballylongford, Co. Kerry
Healy, Michael	22/09/1915		Glenbeigh, Co. Kerry
Healy, Michael	31/07/1917	India	Listowel, Co. Kerry
Hennessey, Denis	20/07/1916	France	Tralee, Co. Kerry
Hennessey, John	31/07/1917	France	Listowel, Co. Kerry
Herbert, William	18/11/1914	France	Tralee, Co. Kerry
Hickey, John	12/07/1916	France	Rathmore, Co. Kerry
Hickey, Timothy	06/07/1915	France	Rathmore, Co. Kerry
Hickey, William	26/06/1916	France	Rathmore, Co. Kerry
Higgins, Dan	08/09/1914		Co. Kerry
Holland, Michael	09/05/1916	France	Kenmare, Co. Kerry
Holland, Patrick	15/11/1914	France	Kenmare, Co. Kerry

Horan, Thomas	05/11/1915		Killarney, Co. Kerry
Hunt, Hamo	15/04/1918	France	Killorglin, Co. Kerry
Hunter, Duncan	19/06/1916	France	Tarbert, Co. Kerry
Hurley, Patrick	30/09/1915	France	Tralee, Co. Kerry
Hussey, John	03/09/1916	France	Sneem, Co. Kerry
Hutton, Thomas	21/08/1915	Gallipoli	Glendermott, Co. Kerry
Johnston, Myles	06/09/1916	France	Killorglin, Co. Kerry
Johnston, Paul	09/05/1915	France	Killarney, Co. Kerry
Keane, James	05/09/1915	Gallipoli	Cahirciveen, Co. Kerry
Keating, Michael	25/03/1915	France	Cahirciveen, Co. Kerry
Keating, Patrick	27/04/1915	Gallipoli	Cahirciveen, Co. Kerry
Leighton, Michael Joseph	14/09/1914	France	Cahirciveen, Co. Kerry
Kelliher, John William	12/10/1917	France	Roxborough, Co. Kerry
Kelly, Francis	06/11/1914	France	Listowel, Co. Kerry
Kelly, Francis	05/10/1918	France	Tralee, Co. Kerry
Kelly, Patrick	25/06/1915	Gallipoli	Tullamore, Co. Kerry
Kelly, Simon	26/09/1916	France	Waterville, Co. Kerry
Kelly, Timothy	22/03/1918	France	Tralee, Co. Kerry
Kennedy, Thomas E.	09/10/1917	France	Dingle, Co. Kerry
King, James	01/12/1917	France	Cahirciveen, Co. Kerry
Kissane, Maurice	15/09/1916	France	Ballbunion, Co. Kerry
Kissane, Patrick	21/03/1918	France	Ardfert, Co. Kerry
Kitchener of Khartoum, Herbert Horatio	05/06/1916		Co. Kerry
Laide, Philip	27/11/1915	Gallipoli	Tralee, Co. Kerry
Lammett, Thomas	16/07/1916	France	Killarney, Co. Kerry

Lane, James	28/07/1916	France	Tralee, Co. Kerry
Langan, John	08/12/1914	France	Tralee, Co. Kerry
Larkin, David	09/09/1916	France	Listowel, Co. Kerry
Leahy, Jeremiah	10/01/1918	France	Lixnaw, Co. Kerry
Leahy, Patrick D.	21/08/1918	France	Brosna, Castleisland, Co. Kerr
Leane, Michael	01/09/1916	France	Lixnaw, Co. Kerry
Leary, Daniel	29/07/1916	France	Tuosist, Kenmare, Co. Kerr
Leen, Daniel	21/03/1918	France	Lixnaw, Co. Kerry
Leen, Stephen	31/07/1917	France	Dirtane, Co. Kerry
Liston, John	08/03/1915	France	Tarbert, Co. Kerry
Long, Patrick	07/12/1916	France	Duagh, Co. Kerry
Long, Patrick	28/08/1918	France	Dingle, Co. Kerry
Long, William	17/09/1916	France	Dingle, Co. Kerry
Lucey, Timothy	17/09/1916	France	Killorglin, Co. Kerry
Lucitt, Joseph	14/04/1918		Tralee, Co. Kerry
Lynch, Michael J.	13/09/1916	France	Tralee, Co. Kerry
Lynch, Daniel	14/11/1914	France	Ballyduff, Co. Kerry
Lyons, John	03/02/1918		Castlemaine, Co. Kerry
Lyons, John	22/08/1917	France	Tralee, Co. Kerry
Lyons, Patrick	07/12/1916	France	Duagh, Co. Kerry
Magee, James	27/11/1917	France	Killarney, Co. Kerry
Mahoney, John	04/10/1915	Gallipoli	Tralee, Co. Kerry
Mahoney, John	03/09/1916	France	Castleisland, Co. Kerry
Mansfield, Joseph	27/09/1918	France	Driminamore, Co. Kerry
McAuliffe, Michael	07/09/1916	Salonika	Listowel, Co. Kerry
McAuliffe, Thomas	17/04/1916	France	Castleisland, Co. Kerry

McCarthy, Daniel	14/12/1916	France	Dingle, Co. Kerry
McCarthy, Daniel	12/04/1917	France	Tralee, Co. Kerry
McCarthy, Daniel	09/10/1917	France	Tralee, Co. Kerry
McCarthy, Florence	14/05/1915		Tralee, Co. Kerry
McCarthy, John	14/08/1915	Gallipoli	Castleisland, Co. Kerry
McCarthy, Justin Shine	20/07/1916	France	Annascaul, Co. Kerry
McCarthy, Michael	11/03/1916	Mesopotamia	Listowel, Co. Kerry
McCarthy, Patrick	20/07/1916	France	Iveragh, Cahirciveen, Co. Kerry
McCarthy, Patrick	22/03/1918	France	Cahirciveen, Co. Kerry
McColgin, James	13/11/1916	France	Tralee, Co. Kerry
McCracken, Wilson	12/10/1918	France	Listowel, Co. Kerry
McEligott, Paul	12/08/1917	Africa	Listowel, Co. Kerry
McElligott, Michael	26/05/1915	Gallipoli	Tralee, Co. Kerry
McGillicuddy, Eugene	09/06/1917	France	Farranfore, Co. Kerry
McGillicuddy, Daniel	16/06/1916	France	Tralee, Co. Kerry
McGillicuddy, Jeremiah	21/08/1916	France	Valencia, Co. Kerry
McGrane, Richard	28/06/1915	Gallipoli	Tralee, Co. Kerry
McKay, Michael	18/04/1916	Mesopotamia	Killarney, Co. Kerry
McKenna, Jeremiah	16/12/1917	France	Ballymcelligott, Co. Kerry
McKenna, John	15/09/1916	France	Milltown, Co. Kerry
McKenna, John	13/09/1916	France	Ballinvoher, Co. Kerry
McLoughlin, Fred	16/06/1917	France	Killarney, Co. Kerry
McQuinn, Patrick J.	02/07/1916	France	Abbeydorney, Co. Kerry
Meara, Michael	15/08/1915	Gallipoli	Firies, Co. Kerry
Meehan, Richard	02/06/1917	France	Kells, Co. Kerry
Metherell, John	30/11/1917	France	Killarney, Co. Kerry

Mitchell, Michael George	18/04/1915	France	Ballylongford, Co. Kerry
Moran, Roger	09/05/1915	France	Tralee, Co. Kerry
Moriarty, Denis	15/11/1915	Gallipoli	Tralee, Co. Kerry
Moriarty, Michael	18/07/1916	France	Tralee, Co. Kerry
Morris, John	04/05/1916	France	Glenmackee, Co. Kerry
Moynihan, Daniel	13/03/1916	France	Killarney, Co. Kerry
Moynihan, Daniel	09/09/1916	France	Glenflesk, Co. Kerry
Moynihan, Denis	27/04/1915	Gallipoli	Castleisland, Co. Kerry
Murphy, Cornelius	31/07/1917	France	Castleisland, Co. Kerry
Murphy, Cornelius	25/08/1917	France	Killarney, Co. Kerry
Murphy, Maurice	27/08/1914	France	Tralee, Co. Kerry
Murphy, Michael	31/10/1914	France	Castleisland, Co. Kerry
Murphy, Michael	12/11/1914	France	Tralee, Co. Kerry
Murphy, Michael	08/05/1916	France	Listowel, Co. Kerry
Murphy, Mortimer	20/06/1916	France	Tralee, Co. Kerry
Murphy, Patrick	18/10/1918	France	Tralee, Co. Kerry
Murphy, Timothy	12/05/1915	France	Killarney, Co. Kerry
Murphy, Timothy Joseph	16/01/1918	France	Tralee, Co. Kerry
Murray, Robert	12/05/1915		Killnockton, Co. Kerry
Nagle, John	10/05/1915	France	Killarney, Co. Kerry
Nash, John	25/02/1915	France	Sneem, Co. Kerry
Neville, John	28/12/1914	France	Tralee, Co. Kerry
Nicholas, Thomas H.	01/11/1914	France	Killarney, Co. Kerry
Nolan, Gerald James	25/04/1918	France	Tralee, Co. Kerry
Nolan, William Craig	05/08/1916	Turkey	Ballylongford, Co. Kerry

Nolan, Edward	29/06/1916	France	Cahirciveen, Co. Kerry
O'Boyle, William	02/11/1917	France	Ballybunion, Co. Kerry
O'Brien, John	25/09/1915	France	Co. Kerry
O'Brien, Michael	30/01/1915	France	Listowel, Co. Kerry
O'Brien, Michael	07/08/1918	France	Tralee, Co. Kerry
O'Brien, Richard	09/05/1915	France	Lyrecompane, Co. Kerry
O'Brien, Timothy	11/05/1915	France	Tralee, Co. Kerry
O'Callaghan, Daniel	24/03/1918	France	Killarney, Co. Kerry
O'Callaghan, John Patrick	09/04/1918	France	Kells, Co. Kerry
O'Connell, Maurice	21/08/1916	France	Ballybunion, Co. Kerry
O'Connell, Patrick J.	01/11/1914	France	Cordal, Co. Kerry
O'Connell, Timothy	09/08/1915	France	Cahirciveen, Co. Kerry
O'Connor, Daniel	05/12/1916	France	Tralee, Co. Kerry
O'Connor, Denis	27/02/1917	Balkans	Ballyhan, Co. Kerry
O'Connor, Dennis	15/09/1916	France	Killarney, Co. Kerry
O'Connor, Florence	21/03/1918	France	Tralee, Co. Kerry
O'Connor, Jeremiah	26/11/1914	France	Killarney, Co. Kerry
O'Connor, John	13/10/1915	France	Tralee, Co. Kerry
O'Connor, John	12/01/1917	France	Tralee, Co. Kerry
O'Connor, Lawrence	15/04/1916	France	St Mary's, Tralee, Co. Kerry
O'Connor, Patrick	29/02/1916	Mesopotamia	Kenmare, Co. Kerry
O'Connor, Thomas	27/08/1915	Gallipoli	Tralee, Co. Kerry
O'Connor, Thomas	28/06/1917	France	Stradbally, Co. Kerry
O'Connor, Thomas	10/11/1917	France	Killarney, Co. Kerry
O'Connor, Thomas	02/09/1918	France	Tralee, Co. Kerry

O'Connor, Timothy	04/11/1918	France	Tralee, Co. Kerry
O'Dell, William	25/09/1915	France	Listowel, Co. Kerry
O'Donnell, Alexander	02/05/1916	France	Tralee, Co. Kerry
O'Donoghue, Daniel	26/10/1918	France	Killarney, Co. Kerry
O'Grady, James	09/08/1915	Gallipoli	Tralee, Co. Kerry
O'Halloran, Edward	01/09/1915	France	Tralee, Co. Kerry
O'Keefe, Dennis	11/04/1917	France	Killarney, Co. Kerry
O'Leary, Daniel S.	25/09/1916	France	Caherdaniel, Co. Kerry
O'Leary, John	27/08/1914	France	Tralee, Co. Kerry
O'Leary, John	27/08/1914	France	Tralee, Co. Kerry
O'Leary, John Cornelius	07/11/1918		Listry, Co. Kerry
O'Regan, Terence	26/10/1917	France	Tralee, Co. Kerry
O'Reilly, F.M.	28/08/1915	France	Lissivigeen, Co. Kerry
O'Shea, Daniel	02/04/1916	France	Killorglin, Co. Kerry
O'Shea, Daniel	11/03/1918	France	Gurthbrack, Co. Kerry
O'Shea, John	12/12/1917	France	Killorglin, Co. Kerry
O'Shea, Michael	26/05/1915	France	Rathmore, Co. Kerry
O'Sullivan, Daniel	09/04/1918	France	Tralee, Co. Kerry
O'Sullivan, Daniel	09/10/1917	France	Tralee, Co. Kerry
O'Sullivan, Daniel	12/11/1914	France	Tralee, Co. Kerry
O'Sullivan, Daniel Joseph	10/07/1918	France	Waterville, Co. Kerry
O'Sullivan, James	30/09/1918	France	Tralee, Co. Kerry
O'Sullivan, Jeremiah	24/05/1918	France	Kenmare, Co. Kerry
O'Sullivan, John	09/05/1915	France	Killarney, Co. Kerry
O'Sullivan, John	28/10/1918		Co. Kerry
O'Sullivan, Michael	02/09/1916	France	Tralee, Co. Kerry

O'Sullivan, Michael	25/10/1916	France	Lees, Co. Kerry
O'Sullivan, Patrick John Lawrence	22/05/1915	France	Killarney, Co. Kerry
O'Sullivan, Terence	18/08/1917	France	Castleisland, Co. Kerry
Oattes, Robert	21/08/1916	France	Tralee, Co. Kerry
Ormsby, John	01/11/1914	France	Ballybunion, Co. Kerry
Pierce, Patrick	28/06/1916	France	Dysart, Co. Kerry
Quinlan, Denis	21/03/1918	France	Kenmare, Co. Kerry
Quinn, Michael	07/06/1917	France	Co. Kerry
Quirke, James	10/11/1917	France	Dingle, Co. Kerry
Radford, Charles William	05/07/1916	France	Waterville, Co. Kerry
Raymond, William	01/10/1917	France	Ballymullen, Tralee, Co. Kerry
Reidy, Michael	26/04/1915	Gallipoli	Co. Kerry
Reynolds, William	09/02/1915		Tralee, Co. Kerry
Riordan, Eugene	28/08/1918	France	Tralee, Co. Kerry
Riordan, Maurice	15/09/1916	France	Kielduff, Co. Kerry
Roberts, Robert	15/07/1916	France	Killarney, Co. Kerry
Roche, John	09/09/1916	France	Tralee, Co. Kerry
Roche, Michael	15/08/1916	Gallipoli	Tralee, Co. Kerry
Rock, Patrick	25/06/1916	France	Cahirciveen, Co. Kerry
Rohan, Thomas	13/11/1915	Gallipoli	St John's, Tralee, Co. Kerry
Rorke, George	20/08/1917	France	Caragh, Co. Kerry
Scanlan, James	06/01/1918	India	Tralee, Co. Kerry
Seeler, Cornelius	29/06/1915	Gallipoli	Co. Kerry
Shanahan, Patrick	28/06/1915	Gallipoli	Portmagee, Co. Kerry
Sharkey, Edward	27/11/1917	France	Tralee, Co. Kerry

Shea, Daniel	04/10/1918	France	Killorglin, Co. Kerry
Shea, George	11/11/1914	France	Tralee, Co. Kerry
Shea, John	27/08/1914	France	Kells, Co. Kerry
Shea, Michael	09/05/1915	France	Listowel, Co. Kerry
Shea, Thomas	25/04/1915	Gallipoli	Killorglin, Co. Kerry
Sheehan, Daniel	01/07/1916	France	Dromid, Co. Kerry
Sheehan, John	01/07/1916	France	Cahirciveen, Co. Kerry
Sheehan, Morgan	21/02/1917		Tralee, Co. Kerry
Sheehan, Timothy	03/09/1916	France	Killarney, Co. Kerry
Sheehy, Michael	19/07/1918	Salonika	Duagh, Co. Kerry
Sheehy, John	26/08/1914	France	Tralee, Co. Kerry
Sheehy, James	25/09/1918	Salonika	Ballymacelligott, Co. Kerry
Sheehy, James	16/09/1916	France	Tralee, Co. Kerry
Stack, Edward	26/10/1914	France	Listowel, Co. Kerry
Stack, John	22/09/1916	France	Tralee, Co. Kerry
Stack, Michael	08/04/1918	France	Listowel, Co. Kerry
Stimpson, William John	22/09/1918	France	Ballinskelligs, Co. Kerry
Sullivan, Bartholomew	28/06/1918	France	Glenbeigh, Co. Kerry
Sullivan, Christopher	21/08/1915	Gallipoli	Killarney, Co. Kerry
Sullivan, Edmund	17/07/1916		Tralee, Co. Kerry
Sullivan, Eugene	27/09/1915	France	Rathbeg, Co. Kerry
Sullivan, James	30/09/1915	France	Killarney, Co. Kerry
Sullivan, James	01/05/1916	France	Firies, Co. Kerry
Sullivan, James	08/02/1917		Killarney, Co. Kerry
Sullivan, John	09/05/1915	France	Tralee, Co. Kerry
Sullivan, John	21/08/1915	Gallipoli	Killarney, Co. Kerry

Sullivan, John	03/09/1916	France	Tralee, Co. Kerry
Sullivan, John	03/09/1916	France	Tralee, Co. Kerry
Sullivan, John	07/10/1916	France	Killarney, Co. Kerry
Sullivan, John	05/10/1917	France	Listowel, Co. Kerry
Sullivan, John	24/12/1917	Salonika	Farranfore, Co. Kerry
Sullivan, John	30/09/1918	France	Listowel, Co. Kerry
Sullivan, Joseph	05/09/1918	France	Barraduff, Co. Kerry
Sullivan, Michael	26/08/1914	France	Killorglin, Co. Kerry
Sullivan, Michael	16/11/1914	France	Cahirciveen, Co. Kerry
Sullivan, Michael	09/05/1915	France	Cahirciveen, Co. Kerry
Sullivan, Michael	08/08/1915	Gallipoli	Killarney, Co. Kerry
Sullivan, Michael	27/04/1916	France	Sneem, Co. Kerry
Sullivan, Michael	04/09/1916	France	Killarney, Co. Kerry
Sullivan, Michael	08/09/1916	France	Glenflesk, Co. Kerry
Sullivan, Michael	15/09/1916	France	Tralee, Co. Kerry
Sullivan, Michael	26/09/1917		Lixnaw, Co. Kerry
Sullivan, Robert	08/08/1918	France	Castleisland, Co. Kerry
Sullivan, Patrick	24/08/1916	France	Tralee, Co. Kerry
Sullivan, Patrick	08/09/1916	France	Waterville, Co. Kerry
Sullivan, Thomas	14/08/1917	France	Sneem, Co. Kerry
Sullivan, Timothy	02/08/1917	France	Rath Co. Kerry
Sullivan, William	21/12/1914	France	Tralee, Co. Kerry
Sweeney, Christopher	20/12/1916	France	Killarney, Co. Kerry
Sweeney, Daniel	29/05/1915	France	Tralee, Co. Kerry
Sweeney, John	09/05/1915	France	Listowel, Co. Kerry
Sweeney, Michael	13/10/1917	France	Kilgarvan, Co. Kerry

Taylor, George Walter	07/11/1914	France	Killarney, Co. Kerry
Thomas, Frederick Charles	16/03/1915	France	Tralee, Co. Kerry
Thompson, Thomas	12/03/1915	France	Co. Kerry
Tracey, Charles Timothy	16/03/1915	France	Tralee, Co. Kerry
Travers, Patrick	23/12/1916		St John's, Tralee, Co. Kerry
Tuohy, James	22/08/1917	France	Kenmare, Co. Kerry
Tuohy, Patrick	16/06/1916		Kenmare, Co. Kerry
Twomey, Daniel	03/09/1916	France	Tralee, Co. Kerry
Wallace, John Aloysius	11/05/1917	France	Tralee, Co. Kerry
Wallace, William	27/08/1914	France	Tralee, Co. Kerry
Walsh, Michael	08/03/1917	France	Killarney, Co. Kerry
Walsh, Michael	21/08/1916	France	Tralee, Co. Kerry
Walsh, Patrick	25/09/1918	France	Tralee, Co. Kerry
Walsh, Thomas	17/04/1918	France	Dingle, Co. Kerry
Warren, Patrick	12/03/1915	France	Killarney, Co. Kerry
Watts, John George	26/03/1918	France	Tralee, Co. Kerry
Welsh, Patrick	11/11/1915		Castleisland, Co. Kerry
Whitaker, Thomas	26/09/1916	France	Tarbert, Co. Kerry
Wright, William	27/08/1914	France	Tralee, Co. Kerry

APPENDIX 2

Name	Unit	Date of Death	Hometown
Abraham Percy Huggard	3rd Battalion, Canadian Infantry	13/06/1916	Cahirciveen
Albert Edward Locke	1st Battalion, Royal Munster Fusiliers	27/11/1915	Tralee
Alfred Aldworth	14th Battalion, Royal Irish Rifles	16/08/1917	Kenmare
Arthur Albert Murphy	42nd Divisional Train, Army Service Corps	29/11/1917	Tralee
Arthur John Cantwell	'A' Company, 2nd Battalion, Royal Munster Fusiliers	09/05/1915	Tralee
Bartholomew Forde	2nd Battalion, Royal Irish Rifles	11/03/1915	Rathmore
Bartholomew Naylor Flynn	2nd Battalion, Royal Munster Fusiliers	27/08/1914	Tralee
Batt Shea	HMS *Good Hope*	11/01/1914	Glenbeigh
C.J. Murphy	1st Battalion, Royal Munster Fusiliers	20/07/1916	Tralee
Chaloner Francis Trevor Chute	1st Battalion, Royal Munster Fusiliers	27/08/1914	Tralee
Charles Edward Scannell	26th Battalion, Australian Infantry	04/10/1917	Tralee
Charles John Browne	1st Battalion, Connaught Rangers	16/11/1914	Sneem

Charles McCarthy	HMS *Goliath*	13/05/1915	Waterville
Charles Quirke	4th Battalion, Seaforth Highlandes	08/10/1917	Unknown
Christopher Phillips	107th Field Company, Royal Engineers	15/12/1918	Killarney
Cornelius Horgan	1st Battalion, Canterbury Regiment, New Zealand Expeditionary Force	26/07/1917	Gullane
D. O'Leary	6th Battalion, Connaught Rangers	29/07/1916	Kenmare
D.J. Finn	13th Battalion, Canadian Infantry	24/04/1915	Glenbeigh
Daniel Carey	36th Australian Heavy Artillery	11/07/1917	Unknown
Daniel Johnstone	HMS *Bulwark*	26/11/1914	Dingle
Daniel Kissane	3rd Battalion, Otago Regiment, New Zealand Expeditionary Force	15/07/1915	Killorglin
Daniel O'Brien	15th Battalion, Canadian Infantry	22/01/1918	Tralee
Desmond Hilary Quin	5th Battalion, The Queens (Royal West Surrey Regiment)	18/09/1918	Tarbert
E. O'Neill	1st Battalion, Royal Munster Fusiliers	12/09/1918	Ballylongfor
Edward Griffin	Wellington Mounted Rifles, New Zealand Expeditionary Force	09/08/1916	Cahirciveer
Everard Digges-La Touch	2nd Battalion, Australian Infantry	06/08/1915	Milltown
F.J. Maybury	1st Battalion, Royal Munster Fusiliers	05/10/1918	Kenmare
Francis Joseph Dodd	Machine Gun Corps	21/10/1918	Dingle
Frank Leonard Dolton	'C' Company, 2nd Battalion, Royal Munster Fusiliers	21/03/1918	Tralee
George Ernest Knightly Evans	3rd Battalion Leinster Regiment	03/09/1916	Killorglin
George Harding	2nd Battalion, King's Own Yorkshire Light Infantry	28/10/1914	Ballymacthon
George Raymond Hifle	3rd Field Company, Canadian Engineers	05/09/1915	Tralee

Gerald Somerville Yeats Cullen	1st Battalion, Royal Irish Fusiliers	11/04/1917	Ballyheigue
J. Diggin	Royal Marine Labour Corps.	28/09/1918	Tralee
J. Thompson	42nd Battalion, Canadian Infantry	24/03/1917	Killarney
J.H. Greaney	2nd Battalion, Leinster Regiment	14/03/1915	Listowel
Jack Sullivan	2nd Australian Light Horse	01/11/1918	Tralee
James Barrett	HMS *Imperious*	10/12/1914	Tralee
James Burns	HMS *Indefatigable*	31/05/1916	Ballybunion
James Canavan	Royal Munster Fusiliers Labour Corps	Oct-18	Killorglin
James Carr	Otago Regiment, New Zealand Expeditionary Force	13/05/1915	Lisselton
James Carroll	HMS *Flirt*	26/10/1916	Aghamore
James David Gloster	6th Battalion, Royal Dublin Fusiliers	18/11/1918	Molahiffe
James Donoghue	HMS *Laurentic*	25/01/1917	Kilgarvan
James Griffen	3rd Battalion, Canadian Machine Gun Corps	02/10/1918	Annascaul
James Lunney	1st Battalion, Rifle Brigade	13/05/1915	Listowel
James Murphy	2nd Field Company, Royal Engineers	12/10/1918	Kilflynn
James O'Connell	1st Battalion, Royal Munster Fusiliers	09/09/1916	Killarney
James Patrick Doherty	14th Battalion, Canadian Infantry	24/05/1915	Tralee
James Patrick Roche	47th Trench Mortar Battery	07/06/1917	Cahirciveen
James Row	1st Battalion, Black Watch	09/05/1915	Ballyheigue
James Teahan	2nd/6th Battalion, London Regiment	30/09/1917	Unknown
James Travers	2nd Battalion, Otago Regiment, New Zealand Expeditionary Force	15/09/1916	Castleisland

Jeremiah O'Donoghue	2nd Battalion, Royal Munster Fusiliers	10/11/1917	Tralee
John Barry	47th Battalion, Australian Infantry	09/08/1917	Tralee
John Charles Donovan	87th Battalion Canadian Infantry	31/05/1918	Tarbert
John Duggan	SS *Lusitania* (Liverpool)	07/05/1915	Co. Kerry
John Gallagher	1st Battalion, York and Lancaster Regiment	05/02/1915	Killarney
John Huleatt Revington	9th Battalion, Devonshire Regiment	04/09/1916	Tralee
John Joseph Bourke	New Zealand Maori (Pioneer) Battalion	15/09/1916	Gortatlea
John Kissane	1st/9th Battalion, London Regiment	04/05/1917	Kenmare
John McCarthy	7th Battalion, Royal Inniskilling Fusiliers	04/04/1916	Kilgarvan
John McKenna	4th Battalion, Worcestershire Regiment	30/04/1915	Killarney
John Michael Foley	44th Battalion, Australian Infantry	16/04/1918	Rathmore
John Murphy	2nd Battalion, Royal Dublin Fusiliers	23/10/1916	Ardfert
John Murphy	25th Battalion, Australian Infantry	07/10/1915	Tralee
John Neligan	9th Hospital Train, Royal Army Medical Corps	13/06/1917	Dingle
John O'Connell Dodd	2nd Battalion, Royal Munster Fusiliers	07/11/1918	Killorglin
John O'Connor	5th Battalion, Souyh Wales Borders	25/03/1918	Ballyhar
John O'Grady	16th Battalion, Australian Infantry	02/03/1915	Glenbeigh
John O'Halloran	1st Battalion, Royal Munster Fusiliers	08/09/1916	Ballylongfor
John Patrick Reaney	'W' Company, 1st Battalion, Royal Munster Fusiliers	22/03/1918	Tralee

John Riordan	21st Battalion, Australian Infantry	25/10/1917	Tralee
John Shanahan	2nd Battalion, Royal Munster Fusiliers	13/10/1915	Listowel
John William Hurley	1st Battalion, Otago Regiment, New Zealand Expeditionary Force	28/08/1918	Castleisland
M. Coffey	2nd Battalion, Royal Munster Fusiliers	12/11/1914	Lixnaw
Marshall Alfred Hill	1st Battalion Royal Dublin Fusiliers and 7th Battalion Royal Irish Rifles	31/05/1918	Milltown
Maurice Francis Butler	1st Battalion, Otago Regiment, New Zealand Expeditionary Force	07/06/1917	Coolbane
aurice James Collis-Sandes	'B' Company, 11th Battalion Royal Fusiliers	17/02/1917	Tralee
Maurice Reidy	SS Isleworth (London)	30/04/1918	Tralee
ichael Bernard O'Connor	3rd Battalion, Canterbury Regiment, New Zealand Expeditionary Force	05/04/1918	Unknown
Michael Charles Hartnett	Royal Munster Fusiliers	19/09/1917	Kenmare
Michael Curran	HMS Black Prince	31/05/1916	Abbeydorney
Michael Dowling	2nd Regiment, South African Infantry	14/10/1917	Waterville
Michael Flynn	HMS Indefatigable	31/05/1916	Killarney
Michael John Moynihan	8th Battalion, The Kings (Liverpool Regiment)	03/06/1918	Tralee
Michael Lynch	2nd Battalion, Royal Munster Fusiliers	01/06/1916	Tarbert
Michael Meade	1st Battalion, Royal Munster Fusiliers	21/08/1915	Tralee
Michael O'Reilly	11th Battalion, Australian Infantry	20/09/1917	Co. Kerry
Michael O'Shea	2nd Battalion, Royal Munster Fusiliers	09/05/1915	Listowel

Michael Sullivan	9th Battalion, Royal Munster Fusiliers	27/04/1916	Sneem
P.J. Galvin	1st Battalion, The Loyal North Lancashire Regiment	24/03/1917	Abbeydorne
Patrick Henry O'Donnell	50th Battalion, Machine Gun Corps	17/09/1918	Tralee
Patrick Burns	1st Wales Borders	10/11/1917	Sneem
Patrick Doherty	102nd Battalion, Canadian Infantry	21/10/1916	Killorglin
Patrick Finn Walsh	1st Field Company, Australian Engineers.	05/03/1917	Tralee
Patrick Fitzgiggon	2nd Battalion, Royal Munster Fusiliers	27/08/1914	Tralee
Patrick Geehan	2nd Battalion, Canterbury Regiment, New Zealand Expeditionary Force	21/07/1918	Killorglin
Patrick Hickey	No.1 Field Company, New Zealand Engineers	23/11/1916	Castleislan
Patrick McGillicuddy	1st Howitzer Battery, New Zealand Field Artillery	12/06/1918	Farranfor
Patrick Molyneux	Welsh Regiment	21/04/1917	Duagh
Patrick O'Brien	'A' Company, 2nd Battalion, Royal Munster Fusiliers	09/05/1915	Tralee
Patrick O'Connor	HMS *Defence*	31/05/1916	Dingle
Patrick O'Leary	1st/4th Battalion, King's Own Yorkshire Light Infantry	24/09/1916	Farranfor
Patrick O'Sullivan	53rd Battalion, Australian Infantry	01/09/1918	Milltowr
Percy Edward Leahy	York and Lancaster Regiment	17/07/1918	Co. Kerry
Richard Henry Williams	1st Battalion, 3rd New Zealand Rifle Brigade	27/03/1918	Unknowr
Richard O'Neill	Wellington Regiment, New Zealand Expeditionary Force	19/08/1915	Beaufort

Robert Hillard	9th Battalion, Australian Infantry	24/12/1916	Castlegregory
Robert Hudson	Canadian Railway Troops	17/10/1918	Tralee
Robert O'Connor	'A' Company, 2nd Battalion, Leinster Regiment	31/07/1917	Tralee
Ronald Horan	47th Battalion, Australian Infantry	02/11/1917	Unknown
Stephen Joseph Murphy	6th Battalion, Royal Munster Fusiliers	24/10/1917	Tralee
Terence Bowler	1st Battalion, Aukland Regiment, New Zealand Expeditionary Force	10/09/1918	Glenbeigh
Terence Fuller Stokes	82nd Punjabis	07/02/1917	Co. Kerry
Thomas Bennett	1st Battalion, Royal Irish Regiment	13/07/1916	Ballyduff
Thomas Corcoran	1st Battalion, Wellington Regiment, New Zealand Expeditionary Force	30/11/1917	Keel
Thomas Hogan (served as Murphy)	2nd Battalion, Royal Inniskilling Fusiliers	14/05/1917	Tralee
Thomas Kearney	SS *Brodmead* (London)	07/09/1917	Abbeydorney
Thomas Louis Enright	Royal Army Medical Corps	19/03/1918	Listowel
Thomas Mahoney	HMS *Monmouth*	01/11/1914	Ardfert
Thomas McGillycuddy	45th Battalion, Australian Infantry	08/07/1918	Beaufort
Timothy Coffey	20th Battalion, Canadian Infantry	23/04/1917	Killarney
Timothy Dennehy	98th Light Railway Operating Company, Royal Engineers	31/12/1917	Waterville
Timothy O'Brien	59th Battalion, Australian Infantry	09/04/1918	Milltown
Timothy O'Riordan	14th Australian Light Trench Mortar Battery	01/10/1917	Killorglin
W. Burke	5th Canadian Mounted Rifles	1-2/10/1916	Co. Kerry
W. Hawley	24th Battalion, Canadian Infantry	10/10/1918	Co. Kerry

W. Scott	19th Company, Machine Gun Corps	18/04/1918	Dingle
W. Traynor	1st Battalion, Royal Munster Fusiliers	27/08/1914	Tralee
Walter De Courcy Dodd	Royal Flying Corps	31/10/1917	Killorglin
William Christopher Boyd	285th Battalion, Canadian Infantry	06/06/1916	Killarney
William Ernest King	2nd Battalion, Australian Infantry	7-14/08/1915	Kilcoleman
William Gardiner McConnell	Royal Army Medical Corps	13/10/1917	Lisselton
William Hayes	The Queens (West Royal Surrey Regiment)	20/10/1918	Dingle
William Hill	Royal Air Force	06/11/1918	Tralee
William John Meredith	3rd Battalion, Royal Munster Fusiliers	20/02/1915	Currow
William Jones	1st Battalion, Irish Guards	16/03/1917	Listowel
William Littlewood	9th Battalion, York and Lancaster Regiment	09/02/1916	Beaufort
William O'Brien	HMS *Monmouth*	01/11/1914	Annascaul
William Quinn	2nd Battalion, Royal Munster Fusiliers	19/11/1917	Tralee
William Richard Herraghty	Princess Patricia's Canadian Light Infantry	28/09/1918	Dingle

APPENDIX 3

LIST OF OFFICERS FROM KERRY.[181]

Name and Rank	Unit
Lt Baily	Royal Munster Fusiliers
Capt. Bland	Unknown
Maj. Blennerhasset	Unknown
Lt Brennan	Royal Army Medical Corps
Lt Browne	Irish Guards
Lt Browne	Irish Guards
Surgeon Barrett	Royal Navy
Lt Casey	Royal Munster Fusiliers
Capt. Carey	Royal Army Medical Corps
Lt Castlerosse	Irish Guards
Lt-Col. Chute	Royal Munster Fusiliers
Capt. Chute	Manchester Regiment
Lt Chute	Royal Munster Fusiliers
Lt Clery	Royal Field Artillery

Capt. Clements–Finnerty	17th Lancers
Capt. Collis–Sandes	Royal Fusiliers
Lt Counihan	Unknown
Lt-Col. Crane	Yorkshire and Lancashire Regiment
Maj. Crosbie	Royal Munster Fusiliers
Lt-Col. Crosbie	Lancashire Fusiliers
Lt Crosbie	Royal Navy
Lt Cullen	Royal Irish Fusiliers
Surgeon Connell	Royal Navy
Lt Connell	Royal Army Medical Corps
Col. Day	Unknown
Lt Downing	2nd Middlesex Regiment
Capt. Dowling	Leinster Regiment
Lt de Moleyns	Royal Navy
Lt Dodd	Royal Munster Fusiliers
Lt Duffy	Royal Munster Fusiliers
Capt. Eager	Royal Munster Fusiliers
Lt Eager	Royal Irish Fusiliers
Maj. Ennismore	Royal Munster Fusiliers
Lt Evans	Leinster Regiment
Lt Eager	Royal Irish Fusiliers
Lt Fishbourne	Unknown
Lt-Col. Fitzgerald	Unknown
Capt. Fitzgerald	Irish Guards

t-Col. Fitzgerald	Shropshire Light Infantry
apt. Fitzgerald	Intelligence Corps
t Fitzgerald	4th Dragoon Guards
: Fitzgerald	Irish Guards
Midshipman Fitzgerald	Royal Navy
t-Col. Fitzmaurice	Royal Signal Corps
:-Col. Fitzmaurice	Royal Field Artillery
: Fitzmaurice	Royal Munster Fusiliers
apt. Fitzmaurice	Irish Guards
apt. Foley	Royal Munster Fusiliers
Foley	Royal Irish Regiment
Foley	Leinster Regiment
apt. Foley	Royal Irish Regiment
rgeon Fitzgerald	Royal Army Medical Corps
Goodwin	Yorkshire and Lancashire Regiment
Girvin	Royal Irish Fusiliers
Greensdale	Unknown
Greensdale	Unknown
apt. Graham	Durham Light Infantry
aj. Hannafin	Unknown
pt. Hannafin	Unknown
Harrington	Unknown
Co. Hartley	Royal Irish Rifles
Hartley	Unknown

Lt Hewson	Unknown
Capt. Hewson	Yorkshire and Lancashire Regiment
Brig.-Gen. Hickson	Unknown
Lt Hickson	Unknown
Lt Hewson	Yorkshire and Lancashire Regiment
Maj. Hood	Unknown
Lt Hussey	Staffordshire
Capt. Hewson	Royal Munster Fusiliers
Capt. Hewson	Army Service Corps
Capt. Hayes	Royal Army Medical Corps
Lt Keane	Royal Munster Fusiliers
Capt. Kelly	Royal Army Medical Corps
Lt-Col. Kerry	Irish Guards
Lt-Col. McCarthy	Royal Army Medical Corps
Lt McElligot	Royal Munster Fusiliers
Maj. MacGillycuddy	Royal Munster Fusiliers
Lt MacGillycuddy	Royal Munster Fusiliers
Maj. MacGillycuddy	Irish Guards
Capt. MacGillycuddy	Royal Army Medical Corps
Capt. MacGillycuddy	Irish Fusiliers
Capt. Magill	Unknown
Lt Magill	Lancashire Regiment
Lt Madden	Unknown
Lt Pierce	Royal Munster Fusiliers

Capt. Maginn	London Regiment
Capt. Meridith	Royal Munster Fusiliers
Moore	Unknown
Capt. Morris	Unknown
Moriarty	Royal Munster Fusiliers
Bernard	Royal Munster Fusiliers
Murphy	Royal Munster Fusiliers
Murphy	Royal Munster Fusiliers
Murphy	Unknown
Murphy	Unknown
Capt. Nash	Unknown
Capt. Nash	Unknown
Capt. Nagle	Sussex Regiment
-Col. O'Connell	Shropshire Light Infantry
O'Connell	Royal Fusiliers
O'Connell	Royal Navy
O'Connell	Royal Navy
Capt. O'Driscoll	Royal Army Medical Corps
-Col. Palmer	46th Punjabs
Power	Royal Navy
Capt. Perrott	Unknown
Capt. Perrott	Royal Garrison Artilery
-Col. Quill	Yorkshire and Lancashire Regiment
Capt. Quinnell	Unknown

Maj. Quinnell	Unknown
Lt Raymond	Unknown
Lt Revington	Devonshire Regiment
Capt. Roche	Unknown
Lt Roche	Royal Munster Fusiliers
Lt Roche	Royal Munster Fusiliers
Capt. Roche	Royal Army Medical Corps
Lt Roche	Royal Army Medical Corps
Capt. Roche	Unknown
Lt Shea	Royal Munster Fusiliers
Lt Shea	Unknown
Capt. Sherrard	Unknown
Lt Slattery	Royal Munster Fusiliers
Lt Stack	Unknown
Lt Sheehan	Unknown
Capt. Talbot	Royal Field Artillery
Lt Wades	Enniskillen Dragoon Guards
Maj. Walker	Royal Army Medical Corps
Capt. Walsh	Chaplain
Lt-Col. Wadden	Unknown
Surgeon Walsh	Royal Navy
Lt Watson	Royal Navy

APPENDIX 4

LIST OF KERRYMEN WHO SURVIVED THE WAR AND DREW A PENSION, COLLECTED FROM SURVIVING SERVICE AND PENSION RECORDS.[182]

Name	Hometown	Date of Enlistment	Occupation	Unit
Alfred John Shotter	Tralee	Unknown	Unknown	Royal Engineers
Alfred O'Connor	Killarney	Unknown	None	Essex Battery
Alfred O'Connor	Killarney	Unknown	Unknown	Unknown
Andrew Collins	Tralee	09/07/1915	Privateer	Royal Munster Fusiliers
Andrew Collins	Tralee	13/02/1902	Printer	Royal Engineers
Bartholomew Sugrue	Tralee	12/11/1919	Unknown	Irish Guards
Basil Arthur Lockley	Ardfert	17/07/1917	Unknown	Irish Guards
Christopher Bartholomew Murphy	Listowel	17/04/1919	Unknown	Unknown
Cornelius O'Shea	Tralee	18/07/1919	Labourer	Royal Engineers
Cornelius Riordan	Tralee	11/11/1890	Labourer	Royal Munster Fusiliers
Daniel Connor	Killorglin	23/04/1887	Clerk	Unknown

Daniel Duggan	Tralee	17/08/1914	Casual Labourer	Royal Munster Fusilie
Daniel Joseph Barrett	Unknown	05/07/1916	Chemist	Royal Engineers
Daniel Lawlor	Tralee	12/06/1912	Casual Labourer	Unknown
Daniel MacGillicuddy	Caherdaniel	Unknown	Farm Labourer	Royal Garrison Artillery
Daniel McCarthy	Tralee	10/08/1914	Unknown	Royal Munster Fusilie
Daniel O'Connor	Tralee	26/10/1914	Labourer	Royal Munster Fusilie
Daniel O'Shea	Tralee	04/08/1900	Tailor	West Riding Regime
David Dillon	Duagh	08/02/1909	None	Irish Guards
Denis Commane	Tralee	01/09/1891	Labourer	Royal Munster Fusilie
Denis Loughlin	Tralee	26/02/1891	Unknown	Royal Munster Fusilie
Dennis Carroll	Tralee	Unknown	Blacksmith	Unknown
Dennis Carroll	Tralee	14/04/1914	Labourer	Royal Munster Fusilie
Dennis Cronin	Castleisland	07/09/1914	Labourer	Royal Irish Regime
Dennis Donovan	Scartaglen	24/07/1897	Labourer	Royal Munster Fusili
Dennis Manning	Tralee	18/02/1901	Unknown	Unknown
Dennis McKenna	Killarney	02/09/1914	Labourer	Royal Irish Fusilier
Dennis Purcell	Tralee	26/07/1919	Canal Labourer	Royal Munster Fusili
Dennis Purcell	Tralee	17/10/1914	Canal Labourer	Royal Munster Fusili
Edmond Casey	Castleisland	22/05/1914	Labourer	Labour Corps
Edward Blennerhasset	Valencia	10/08/1914	Male Nurse	Royal Army Medic Corps
Edward Broder	Listowel	28/08/1914	Labourer	Royal Munster Fusili

Edward Cain	Listowel	11/08/1914	Clerk	Army Ordnance Corps
Edward Crowley	Unknown	Unknown	Unknown	Unknown
Edward Deasy	Tralee	16/07/1888	Labourer	Royal Munster Fusiliers
Edward Dennehy	Cahersiveen	27/10/1914	Baker	Irish Guards
Edward Fryer	Tralee	24/02/1887	None	Royal Munster Fusiliers
Edward McGann	Tralee	28/09/1903	Photographer	Royal Garrison Regiment
Edward McGann	Tralee	11/11/1887	Unknown	Royal Artillery
dward William Creagh	Tralee	31/01/1894	Unknown	Royal Artillery
Eugene Sullivan	Tralee	17/11/1890	Unknown	Royal Dublin Fusiliers
George Brett	Tralee	Unknown	Tailor	Royal Scots
George Mason	Tralee	22/09/1914	Skilled Labourer	Welsh Regiment
George Parkinson	Tralee	06/05/1898	Clerk	Royal Munster Fusiliers
Harold Arthur Pickett	Tralee	05/09/1914	Packer	The London Regiment
Henry Coffey	Abbeydorney	30/08/1897	Labourer	Royal Artillery
Henry Coffey	Lixnaw	29/01/1915	Unknown	Army Service Corps
Henry Coffey	Tralee	19/09/1914	Labourer	Royal Munster Fusiliers
Henry Gogfrey	Tralee	19/01/1905	Skilled Labourer	Royal Munster Fusiliers
Henry Kenny	Tralee	12/10/1914	Canal Labourer	Royal Munster Fusiliers
Henry Kenny	Tralee	31/08/1895	Labourer	Royal Munster Fusiliers
erbert Francis Huntley	Tralee	15/01/1914	Unknown	Argyll & Sutherland Highlanders
Hugh Bradford	Scartaglen	25/??/1895	Labourer	Royal Artillery

Hugh Cole	Unknown	29/09/1914	Labourer	Royal Artillery
Hugh Cole	Milltown	29/09/1914	Labourer	Royal Irish Fusiliers
James Bell	Unknown	18/??/1907	Labourer	Royal Munster Fusilie
James Canavan	Listowel	16/08/1914	Labourer	Royal Munster Fusilie
James Carroll	Tralee	14/04/1914	Labourer	Royal Artillery Ordnance Corps
James Cournane	Unknown	07/04/1895	Labourer	Royal Artillery
James Hill	Killarney	13/11/1917	Painter	Royal Engineers
James O'Connor	Tralee	05/09/1914	Labourer	Royal Munster Fusilie
James Phillips	Tralee	15/04/1914	Coal Miner	West Yorkshire Regiment
James Phillips	Tralee	16/06/1914	Coal Miner	South Lancashire Regiment
James Plummer	Killarney	18/10/1897	None	North Staffordshire Regiment
James Purcell	Tralee	25/06/1919	Stroeman	Royal Engineers
James Purcell	Tralee	15/11/1898	Labourer	Royal Munster Fusili
James Sullivan	Kilcrohane	23/03/1903	Labourer	Royal Garrison Artillery
James Walsh	Tralee	05/09/1914	Labourer	Unknown
Jeremiah Clifford	Tralee	03/10/1882	Labourer	Unknown
Jeremiah Donohue	Killarney	26/03/1891	Labourer	Royal Engineers
Jeremiah Griffen	Tralee	02/08/1905	Labourer	Royal Munster Fusil
Jeremiah Looney	Tralee	16/04/1909	Groom	Royal Dublin Fusili

Jeremiah O'Connor	Tralee	02/07/1909	Telegraphist	London Army Troops
Jeremiah O'Regan	Tralee	17/09/1914	Labourer	Unknown
Jeremiah O'Sullivan	Cahersiveen	23/09/1914	Baker	Royal Munster Fusiliers
Jeremiah O'Sullivan	Faranfore	18/02/1889	Labourer	Royal Munster Fusiliers
Jeremiah O'Sullivan	Tralee	05/09/1914	Labourer	Royal Munster Fusiliers
Jeremiah Prendiville	Tralee	19/04/1915	Unknown	Irish Guards
Jeremiah Sheehy	Tralee	06/12/1899	Tailor	9th Hussars
John Barry	Listowel	13/08/1919	Stroeman	Unknown
John Barry	Listowel	19/09/1914	Labourer	Royal Munster Fusiliers
John Barry	Killarney	22/02/1901	Chemical	Unknown
John Black	Tarbert	??/08/1914	Clerk	Royal Field Artillery
John Burke	Glenbeigh	07/09/1914	Labourer	Royal Munster Fusiliers
John Carew	Tralee	03/09/1914	Caster	Royal Irish Regiment
John Coffey	Duagh	03/04/1894	Tinsmith	Royal Munster Fusiliers
John Cole	Tralee	29/10/1902	Waiter	Royal Munster Fusiliers
John Conboy	Tralee	24/05/1919	Policeman	Royal Engineers
John Connor	Tralee	03/09/1914	Caster	Royal Irish Fusiliers
John Connor	Tralee	07/10/1914	Bricklayer	Royal Garrison Artillery
John Connors	Tralee	10/04/1912	Labourer	Royal Munster Fusiliers
John Connors	Tralee	21/11/1894	Labourer	Royal Munster Fusiliers
John Cournane	Tralee	Unknown	None	Royal Munster Fusiliers

John Cremin	Killarney	05/09/1900	Shoe cobbler	Army Service Corps
John Cronin	Milltown	19/02/1906	Labourer	Dragoon Guards
John Crowley	Killarney	25/08/1914	Coal Miner	Royal Garrison Artillery
John Fitzgerald	Tralee	28/12/1911	Labourer	Royal Munster Fusiliers
John Fitzgerald	Tralee	28/06/1911	Clerk	Royal Munster Fusiliers
John Foley	Tralee	25/03/1916	Farm Labourer	Royal Munster Fusiliers
John Ford	Coolcoslough	31/08/1914	Baker	Unknown
John Franklin Brown	Tralee	13/03/1897	Labourer	Seaforth Highlanders
John Halloran	Tralee	11/01/1898	Labourer	Leinster Regiment
John Higgins	Tralee	19/12/1902	Labourer	Royal Munster Fusiliers
John McCarthy	Tralee	25/08/1914	Oil Maker	Irish Guards
John McDonnell	Tralee	12/10/1898	Shoemaker	Royal Munster Fusiliers
John McDonnell	Tralee	05/10/1914	Shoemaker	Royal Munster Fusiliers
John McGelligot	Ardfert	21/08/1914	Labourer	Royal Munster Fusiliers
John McGelligot	Ardfert	21/01/1894	Labourer	Royal Munster Fusiliers
John Murphy	Tralee	24/06/1898	None	Royal Munster Fusiliers
John Nagle	Tralee	20/08/1914	Labourer	Royal Munster Fusiliers
John Nagle	Tralee	12/11/1894	Labourer	Royal Munster Fusiliers
John O'Brien	Geeneguilla	26/08/1918	Labourer	Royal Irish Regiment
John O'Connell	Listowel	09/07/1912	Farm Labourer	Royal Munster Fusiliers
John O'Connor	Tralee	17/01/1902	Labourer	Royal Army Medical Corps

John O'Grady	Tralee	16/01/1914	Tinsmith	Royal Irish Regiment
John O'Grady	Tralee	14/07/1914	Groom	Leinster Regiment
John O'Leary	Tralee	21/07/1907	Billiard Maker	Connaught Rangers
John Patrick Kaye	Tralee	09/04/1895	None	Leinster Regiment
John Purcell	Derrymore	15/05/1911	Labourer	Royal Regiment of Artillery
John Shea	Tralee	09/11/1890	Labourer	Royal Artillery
John Shea	Tralee	03/01/1902	Billiard Maker	Royal Garrison Regiment
John Timoney	Tralee	06/12/1899	Labourer	Corps of Lancers of the Line
John Timoney	Tralee	04/07/1916	Labourer	5th Lancers
John West	Tralee	05/08/1909	Farm Labourer	Connaught Rangers
Joseph Collins	Tralee	16/09/1914	Fireman	South Lancer
Joseph Dennehy	Castlemain	31/12/1908	Fisherman	Royal Munster Fusiliers
oseph Henry Collett	Unknown	11/06/1909	Glass fitter	London Regiment
Martin Carmody	Tralee	29/10/1902	Tailor	Connaught Rangers
Martin Carmody	Knockanure	11/07/1919	Labourer	Royal Army Medical Corps
Matin Walsh	Tralee	11/08/1914	Painter	Royal Munster Fusiliers
Maurice Carroll	Abbeydorney	27/11/1897	Labourer	Royal Munster Fusiliers
Maurice Connor	Tralee	17/09/1874	None	Unknown
Maurice Curtin	Tralee	19/08/1920	Labourer	Royal Irish Regiment

Maurice Fitzgerald	Tralee	10/07/1911	Labourer	Royal Munster Fusilier
Maurice Fitzgerald	Tralee	12/02/1912	Labourer	Royal Munster Fusilier
Maurice Frant	Tralee	18/08/1884	Labourer	North Staffordshire Regiment
Maurice Frant	Tralee	03/10/1914	Store Keeper	Labour Corps
Maurice Murphy	Tralee	29/07/1919	Labourer	Hampshire Regiment
Maurice Murphy	Tralee	21/12/1892	Labourer	Royal Munster Fusilier
Michael Ahern	Tralee	04/01/1912	Roofer	Royal Engineers
Michael Barrett	Tralee	Unknown	Labourer	Unknown
Michael Brennen	Tralee	19/06/1919	Engine Driver	Royal Engineers
Michael Brennen	Killarney	02/09/1919	Miner	Military Foot Police
Michael Canty	Listowel	23/05/1911	Labourer	Connaught Rangers
Michael Carroll	Listowel	23/04/1890	Labourer	Royal Artillery
Michael Casey	Killarney	19/05/1913	Unknown	Unknown
Michael Casey	Killorglin	23/08/1915	Plate Layer	Royal Engineers
Michael Clancy	Kilkee	13/10/1917	Labourer	Royal Field Artillery
Michael Connor	Dingle	04/11/1914	Labourer	Cheshire Regiment
Michael Conway	Tralee	09/05/1902	Labourer	Royal Munster Fusilie
Michael Crowley	Tralee	11/04/1894	Carpenter	Royal Engineers
Michael Cummin	Killarney	Unknown	Labourer	Unknown
Michael Dee	Listowel	07/04/1914	Farmer	Irish Guards
Michael Donnelly	Tralee	31/01/1898	Labourer	Royal Munster Fusilie

Michael Fizgerald	Ardfert	03/07/1919	Labourer	Royal Garrison Artillery
Michael Flahive	Tralee	04/09/1895	None	Wiltshire Regiment
Michael Flahive	Tralee	05/06/1911	Musician	Royal Munster Fusiliers
Michael Herrity	Tralee	10/10/1904	Labourer	Royal Munster Fusiliers
Michael Joseph Murphy	Tralee	03/01/1899	Butler	Royal Artillery
Michael Lyne	Ardfert	19/02/1895	Labourer	Royal Munster Fusiliers
Michael Moriarty	Rathmore	11/08/1914	Postman	Royal Munster Fusiliers
Michael Moroney	Tralee	02/10/1909	Labourer	Royal Munster Fusiliers
Michael Moroney	Tralee	02/03/1910	Farm Labourer	Royal Munster Fusiliers
Michael Murphy	Tralee	22/10/1901	Labourer	Royal Munster Fusiliers
Michael Murphy	Tralee	16/07/1919	Labourer	Liverpool Regiment
Michael O'Shea	Tralee	28/09/1914	Labourer	Royal Munster Fusiliers
Michael O'Shea	Tralee	28/09/1914	Labourer	Royal Munster Fusiliers
Michael O'Shea	Tralee	18/10/1919	Storeman	Unknown
Michael O'Shea	Tralee	22/01/1920	Labourer	Royal Fusiliers
Michael Sheehan	Killarney	14/03/1901	Barman	Royal Rifle Corps
Michael Sullivan	Tralee	26/08/1914	Miller	Leinster Regiment
Michael Sullivan	Sneem	28/08/1914	Labourer	Royal Irish Fusiliers
Patrick Carmody	Tralee	22/08/1903	Labourer	Royal Munster Fusiliers
Patrick Casey	Dingle	11/11/1908	Seaman	Grenadier Guards

Patrick Casey	Waterville	19/10/1917	Labourer	Royal Field Artillery
Patrick Connor	Tralee	26/05/1919	Labourer	Labour Corps
Patrick Devine	Tralee	29/07/1890	Labourer	Royal Munster Fusilier
Patrick Devine	Tralee	20/10/1902	Labourer	Royal Garrison Regiment
Patrick Donnelly	Tralee	11/11/1902	Labourer	Royal Munster Fusilier
Patrick Ferris	Listowel	26/08/1907	Farm Labourer	Irish Guards
Patrick Ferris	Tralee	26/08/1914	Labourer	Royal Welsh Regiment
Patrick Healy	Tralee	04/01/1904	Labourer	Royal Munster Fusilie
Patrick Horan	Tralee	27/01/1888	Labourer	Royal Munster Fusilie
Patrick Horan	Tralee	03/10/1901	Labourer	Royal Garrison Regiment
Patrick Horan	Tralee	09/01/1909	Labourer	Royal Garrison Regiment
Patrick Horan	Tralee	09/09/1914	Labourer	Labour Corps
Patrick Joseph Black	Dingle	04/09/1903	Clerk	Royal Regiment o Artillery
Patrick Joseph Quane	Ardfert	05/05/1913	Farm Labourer	Royal Army Medic Corps
Patrick Mack	Tralee	09/04/1919	Labourer	Royal Munster Fusilie
Patrick McCarthy	Tralee	01/09/1914	Labourer	Royal Munster Fusili
Patrick McCarthy	Tralee	08/09/1919	Stonemason	Unknown
Patrick McKenna	Tralee	28/12/1892	Labourer	Royal Munster Fusili
Patrick McLoughlin	Duagh	01/05/1893	Labourer	Labour Corps

Patrick McLoughlin	Tralee	20/12/1910	Labourer	Royal Regiment of Artillery (Reserve)
Patrick Murtagh	Tralee	12/09/1894	Teacher	Royal Munster Fusiliers
Patrick Murtagh	Tralee	13/05/1907	Unknown	Royal Engineers
Patrick O'Connor	Tralee	13/12/1894	Tailor	Connaught Rangers
Patrick O'Connor	Tralee	21/12/1904	Tailor	East Lancashire
Patrick O'Sullivan	Tralee	15/11/1898	Labourer	Royal Munster Fusiliers
Patrick Stack	Duagh	22/01/1895	Labourer	Royal Munster Fusiliers
Patrick Stack	Duagh	14/08/1914	Labourer	Royal Munster Fusiliers
Patrick Sullivan	Tralee	23/08/1914	Labourer	Royal Munster Fusiliers
Patrick Sullivan	Killorglin	07/09/1914	Labourer	Royal Dublin Fusiliers
Patrick Twohey	Tralee	4/12/1889	Unknown	Unknown
Patrick Walsh	Tralee	03/12/1913	Baker	4th Dragoon Guards
Patrick Walsh	Tralee	08/08/1914	Labourer	Leinster Regiment
Pete Paul Fitzel	Ballylongford	14/07/1917	Toolmaker	Scots Guards
Peter Glover	Tralee	08/07/1920	Labourer	Leinster Regiment
Peter Moran	Fenit	04/12/1903	Labourer	Royal Munster Fusiliers
Richard Barrett	Killorglin	27/11/1915	Painter	Connaught Rangers
Richard Barrett	Killarney	02/09/1919	Painter	Army Ordnance Corps
Richard McAuliffe	Brosna	13/05/1895	Clerk	Royal Engineers
Robert Harford	Tralee	21/07/1882	None	Unknown
Robert Harford	Tralee	15/01/1896	Musician	Rifle Brigade

Robert Hope	Killarney	20/08/1914	Labourer	Unknown
Robert McKee	Ballylongford	09/02/1914	Labourer	Royal Regiment of Artillery
Rowland Abernethy	Tralee	10/10/1900	Clerk	Army Service Corp
Stanley Groves	Tralee	03/07/1914	Baker	Royal Munster Fusilie
Thomas Bower	Tralee	12/09/1914	Painter	Royal Munster Fusilie
Thomas Cleary	Dingle	28/02/1917	Seaman	Royal Engineers
Thomas Collins	Tralee	10/07/1905	Unknown	Royal Engineers
Thomas Collins	Tralee	28/08/1914	Unknown	Unknown
Thomas Crean	Tralee	08/??/1888	Clerk	Royal Engineers
Thomas Crean	Tralee	20/08/1894	Clerk	Royal Dublin Fusilie
Thomas Fitzgerald	Tralee	04/07/1919	Baker	Army Service Corp
Thomas Fitzgibbon	Tralee	03/08/1892	None	Royal Munster Fusilie
Thomas Foley	Tralee	11/07/1885	Labourer	Royal Munster Fusili
Thomas Foley	Tralee	25/09/1902	Labourer	Royal Garrison Regiment
Thomas Foley	Tralee	12/09/1904	Labourer	Royal Munster Fusil
Thomas Foley	Tralee	05/09/1914	Labourer	Royal Munster Fusil
Thomas Galvin	Tralee	11/09/1914	Labourer	Royal Fusiliers
Thomas Garvey	Tralee	30/08/1892	Labourer	Grenadier Guards
Thomas Hogan	Killarney	08/05/1894	Labourer	Royal Munster Fusil
Thomas Hogan	Killarney	19/09/1914	Coachman	Royal Munster Fusil

Thomas Neligan	Duagh	26/08/1914	Labourer	Highland Light Infantry
Thomas Patrick Grant	Tralee	27/10/1919	Engine Driver	Royal Army Medical Corps
Thomas Spillane	Tralee	08/12/1903	Labourer	Leinster Regiment
Thomas Walsh	Tralee	30/10/1884	Labourer	Royal Munster Fusiliers
Thomas Walsh	Tralee	25/07/1919	Labourer	Hampshire Regiment
Tim Hanafin	Tralee	12/08/1914	Labourer	Royal Munster Fusiliers
Timothy Callaghan	Tralee	27/12/1897	Labourer	Leinster Regiment
Timothy Collins	Dingle	02/07/1919	Farm Labourer	Royal Engineers
Timothy Fitzgerald	Tralee	25/09/1902	Labourer	Royal Munster Fusiliers
Timothy Fitzgerald	Tralee	25/09/1902	Labourer	Royal Munster Fusiliers
Timothy Healy	Killarney	05/09/1914	Blacksmith	Royal Engineers
Timothy O'Leary	Killarney	02/11/1912	Farm Labourer	Irish Guards
Timothy O'Shea	Tralee	04/09/1914	Labourer	Cheshire Regiment
Walter Costello	Castleisland	??/03/1894	Surveyor	Royal Engineers
Walter Day	Tralee	29/01/1903	Labourer	Royal Regiment of Artillery, Horse and Field Artillery
Walter William John Hardy	Tralee	22/07/1896	Sailor	South Staffordshire Regiment
William Christopher Stevens	Tralee	19/03/1915	Labourer	Royal Munster Fusiliers
William Christopher Stevens	Tralee	06/04/1918	Clerk	Royal Marines

William Christopher Stevens	Tralee	20/10/1920	Clerk	Royal Army Ordnance Corps
William Dunn	Tralee	22/08/1914	Labourer	Cameron Highlanders
William James Stevenson	Tralee	Unknown	Drummer	South Staffordshire Regiment
William Knight	Tralee	11/10/1901	Groom	Unknown
William Knight	Tralee	17/02/1914	Labourer	Hampshire Regiment
William Leslie	Killarney	15/01/1910	Farmer	Irish Guards
William Mangan	Killorglin	20/11/1919	School Teacher	Royal Army Service Corps
William Martin Allen	Unknown	29/09/1882	None	Royal Artillery
William Murphy	Unknown	05/03/1913	Clerk	Somerset Regiment
William Slattery	Tralee	25/07/1916	Labourer	Connaught Rangers
William Woolridge	Tralee	04/09/1914	Painter	Royal Berkshire Regiment

APPENDIX 5

Name	Role in War of Independence
Jack Sullivan	Post Office employee, who passed on military communications to the IRA.
Jim Duggan	Radio officer in the army and occasional driver for Tom McEllistrim and Johnny O'Connor.
Tommy Wall	Member of IRA in Tralee and killed by the Black and Tans on 2 November 1920.
apt. Tyrell O'Mahony	Captain in the Royal Munster Fusiliers. Originally from Mayo, he passed on information to the IRA.
Jim Duffy	Worked for the RIC and spied for the IRA.
Col. Berkley	Commander in Ballymullen Barracks. He despised the Black and Tans and passed on information to Tim Kennedy, an IRA intelligence officer.

Phil Roche	Radio operator in Ballymullen Barracks. He supplied intelligence and arms to the IRA.
Cpl Perry	Radio operator who supplied the IRA with intelligence and famously showed Christy O'Connor of the IRA around Ballymullen Barracks.
Tom Kennelly	Elected leader of the of a newly established North Kerry flying column on 30 January 1921.
Jim Coffey	A key member of the Ballymac Battalion of the IRA under Thomas McEllistrim.
James Cornelius Healy	A veteran sniper and member of Boherbee section of the IRA under John Joe Sheehy. Famously killed Maj. Mackinnon at Tralee Golf Course.
Fr William Behan	Former Army Chaplin. Organised a petition, declaring that the Kerry No.1 Brigade was not doing enough. He had to be protected by the IRA.

APPENDIX 6

Paddy Foley	Former member of the Royal Munster Fusiliers. He attempted to give up members of the IRA using his brother Mick Foley and cousin Tim Kennedy, who were IRA officers.
John 'Boxer' O'Mahony	Killed by the Boherbee section of the IRA; not for being an ex-serviceman but for spying.
Denny O'Loughlin	Former serviceman who spied for the RIC and was killed in Knightly's Bar. His name was given up by John O'Mahony.
Fr E.H. Collins	Former Chaplin and member of the Dominican Order. He was killed with the permission of the Irish Dominican Order for his allegiance to the British.
John 'Cousy' Fitzgerald	Former serviceman and prominent Redmond and National Volunteer supporter. His name was given up by O'Mahony as a spy. He was shot through the eyes.

BIBLIOGRAPHY

NEWSPAPERS

Irish Independent
The Irish Times
Kerry Evening Post
The Kerry News
The Kerry Sentinel
The Kerryman
The Liberator

ARCHIVAL INFORMATION

1911 Census.
British Army Pension Records, WO 364, National Archives, Kew.
British Army Service Records, WO 363, National Archives, Kew.
Dáil Éireann – Volume 19 – 29 March 1927, Private Business – The Merrion
    Square (Dublin) Bill, 1927.
Ordnance Survey Office, Southampton, 1906.
Ordnance Survey, Historic Map Series, 2008.
Seanad Éireann – Volume 8 – 09 March 1917, The Merrion Square (Dublin) Bill,
    1927 – Second Stage.

THESES

Martin, Thomas F., *Politics, Society, Economics & Recruitment in Kerry during World
    War I* (MA Thesis: UCC, 2005).
Staunton, Martin, *The Royal Munster Fusiliers in the Great War, 1914-19,* (MA Thesis:
    UCD, 1986).

BOOKS

Barry, Tom, *Guerrilla Days in Ireland* (Anvil: Dublin, 1949).

Bartlett, Thomas & Keith, Jeffery, *A Military History of Ireland* (Cambridge University Press: Cambridge, 1996).

Bew, Paul, *Conflict and Conciliation 1890-1910: Parnellites and Radical Agrarians* (Oxford University Press: Oxford, 1987).

Bort, Eberhard, *Commemorating Ireland, History, Politics, Culture* (Irish Academic Press: Dublin, 2004).

Bowen, Desmond & Jean, *Heroic Option* (Pen and Sword Books Ltd: London, 2005).

Bowmann, Timothy, *The Irish Regiments in The Great War: Discipline and Morale* (Manchester University Press: Manchester, 2004).

Chandler, Malcolm, *The Home Front 1914-18* (Harcourt Heinemann: London, 2002).

Churchill, Winston, *The Great War Volume One* (George Newnes Ltd: London).

Churchill, Winston, *The Great War Volume Two* (George Newnes Ltd: London).

Coogan, Tim Pat, *Ireland in the Twentieth Century* (Hutchinson: London, 2003).

Cooper, Bryan, *The Tenth (Irish) Division in Gallipoli* (Herbert Jenkins: London, 1918).

Denman, Terrence, *Ireland's Unknown Soldiers: The 16ᵗʰ (Irish) Division In The Great War, 1914-1918* (Irish Academic Press Ltd: Dublin, 1922).

Doherty, Gabriel & Keogh, Dermot, *1916 The Long Revolution* (Mercier Press: Cork, 2007).

Dungan, Myles, *Irish Voices from the Great War* (Irish Academic Press: Dublin, 1995).

Ferguson, Niall, *The Pity of War 1914-1918* (Penguin: London, 1999).

Fitz Patrick, D., *The Two Irelands 1912-1939* (Oxford University Press: Oxford, 1998).

Fitzpatrick, D., *Ireland and the First World War* (Trinity History Workshop: Dublin, 1986).

Foster, R.F., *Modern Ireland 1600-1972* (Penguin: London, 1988).

Fraser, Murray, *John Bull's Other Homes: State Housing and British Policy in Ireland, 1883-1922* (Liverpool University Press: Liverpool, 1996).

Gregory, Adrian & Paseta, Senia, *Ireland and the Great War: A War to Unite us All?* (Manchester University Press: Manchester, 2002).

Hamilton, General Sir Ian, *Gallipoli Diary Volume I* (George H. Doran Company: New York, 1920).

Hamilton, General Sir Ian, *Gallipoli Diary Volume II* (George H. Doran Company: New York, 1920).

Harris, Henry, *The Irish Regiments in the First World War* (Mercier Press: Cork, 1968).

Hennessey, Thomas, *Dividing Ireland: World War One and Partition* (Routledge, 1998).

Henry, William, *Forgotten Heroes, Galway Soldiers of the Great War 1914-1918* (Mercier Press: Cork, 2007).

Howe, Stephen, *Ireland and Empire: Colonial Legacies in Irish History and Culture* (Oxford University Press: Oxford, 2002).

Jeffery, Keith, *Ireland and the Great War* (Cambridge University Press: Cambridge, 2000).

Jervis, H.S., *The 2nd Munsters in France* (Schull Books: Cork, 1998).

Johnson, Nuala C., *Ireland, The Great War and the Geography of Remembrance* (Cambridge University Press: Cambridge, 2003).

Johnstone, Tom, *Orange, Green & Khaki The Story of the Irish Regiments in the Great War, 1914-18* (Gill & Macmillan: Dublin, 1992).

Kendle, John, *Walter Long, Ireland, and the Union, 1905-1920* (McGill–Queen's University Press: Montreal, 1992).

Keogh, Dermot, *Twentieth-Century Ireland* (Gill & Macmillan: Dublin, 1994).

Kildea, Jeff, *Anzacs and Ireland* (Cork University Press: Cork, 2007).

Lee, J.J., *Ireland 1912-1985 Politics and Society* (Cambridge University Press: Cambridge, 1989).

Lewis, Samuel, *A Topographical Dictionary of Ireland* (S. Lewis & Co.: London, 1837).

Lyons, J.B., *The Enigma of Tom Kettle: Irish Patriot, Essayist, Poet, British Soldier* (Glendale Press: Dublin, 1992).

MacDonagh, Michael, *The Irish At The Front* (Hodder & Stoughton: London, 1916).

MacDonagh, Michael, *The Irish on the Somme* (Hodder & Stoughton: London, 1917).

Martin, Thomas F., *The Kingdom in The Empire, A Portrait of Kerry During World War One* (Nonsuch Publishing: Dublin, 2006).

McMorran, Russell & O'Keeffe, Maurice, *The Old Kerry Journal* (Tralee, 2006).

Moorehead, Alan, *Gallipoli* (Hamish Hamilton: London, 1964).

Murphy, David, *The Irish Brigades 1685-2006* (Four Courts Press: Dublin, 2007).

O'Day, Alan, *Irish Home Rule, 1867-1921* (Manchester University Press: Manchester, 1998).

O'Garda, Cormac, *Ireland: A New Economic History 1780-1939* (Oxford University Press: Oxford, 1995).

O'Day, Alan, & Boyce, David George, *Ireland in Transition, 1867-1921* (Routledge: Dublin, 2004).

Orr, Philip, *Field of Bones: An Irish Division At Gallipoli* (Lilliput Press: Dublin, 2006).

Dooley, Thomas P., *Irishmen or English Soldiers: The Times and World of a Southern Irish Catholic Man (1876-1916) Enlisting in the British Army during The First World War* (Liverpool University Press: Liverpool, 1995).

Parnell Kerr, S., *What The Irish Regiments Have Done* (T. Fisher Unwin Ltd: London, 1916).

Redmond, John E., O'Connor T.P., & Keating, J., *Irish Heroes in the War* (Everett & Co.: London, 1917).

Rickard, Mrs Victor, *The Story of The Munsters At Etreux, Festbert and Rue Du Bois* (Hodder & Stoughton: London, 1918).

Ryle Dwyer, T., *Tans, Terror and Troubles, Kerry's Real Fighting Story 1913-23* (Mercier Press: Cork, 2001).

Simkins, Peter, *Kitchener's Army, The Raising of The New Armies 1914- 1916* (Pen and Sword Books: Barnsley, 1988).